Screamingly Good Food

Screamingly Good Food

Fresh Feasts and Seasonal Meals
to Knock Your Socks Off

Karen Barnaby

Whitecap Books
Vancouver/Toronto

Edited by Elaine Jones
Proofread by Elizabeth McLean
Cover design by Warren Clark
Cover photograph by Greg Athans
Typeset by Warren Clark

Printed and bound in Canada.

Canadian Cataloguing in Publication Data

Barnaby, Karen
    Screamingly good food

    Includes index.
    ISBN 1-55110-619-1

    1. Holiday cookery 2. Cookery. I. Title
TX739.B37 1997   641.5'68   C97-910659-1

For more information on other titles from Whitecap Books, visit our web site at www.whitecap.ca

To my husband, Steven, my true love and
true partner

&

To Hubert Schmid, who showed me how to
see the oak tree in the acorn

Contents

Introduction 1

Spring

Summer

Fall

Winter

Basics and Biscuits 204

Introduction

$\mathcal{W}$e learn the pleasures of celebrations and feasting at an early age. A feast usually involves a ritualized event, and for many of us Christmas is our first such memory. Birthdays are another. Your parents might take you to a favorite place or have your favorite cake and food. My mother always made party sandwiches for mine, with chocolate milk, chocolate cake and vanilla ice cream. I was especially fascinated by the pinwheel sandwiches made from Cheez Whiz with the pimento-stuffed olive in the middle. There were other times that I knew were special and profound. I didn't have the words at the time to express what I felt, but raspberries from the lady up the street who had raspberry bushes, avocados with lime and sugar in late winter, and rhubarb compote every spring made me associate certain foods with certain times of the year. The eating of them seemed unique and special, and now, with an adult view of the past, I know that they truly were. This association has been my ally in creating my own feasts and reasons to feast.

We notice the rain making patterns on the window, the quality of sunlight on certain days. When we have the first great tomato of the season, when the scent in the air changes, the first meal of the year we eat outside, when the last leaf falls—events that make us go "ahh" and "aha." A spectrum of sights, sounds, smells, thoughts and feelings, inspiration and doing, cooking and eating, becomes a part of who we are. This is a book that celebrates all of those moments.

I enjoy traditional feast times, but think it is important to have a personal lexicon of feasts as well. I don't usually eat traditionally because it doesn't strike my fancy or seem practical at the time. In the process, new and different, personal feasts are created. The Feast of the Snow Crab, page 151, is a perfect example, and so is the following, which could be called "A Feast for Two Lives on the Verge of Becoming One."

Imagine two budding chefs, 25 years old, living on Kensington Avenue in Toronto, one of the most interesting urban food markets in North America. The year was 1982 and you could buy live squawking chickens, pigeons and quails in cages, stare at small mountains constructed out of cheese, their

cut faces bulging from their collective weight, eat spicy Jamaican patties from the Patty King, and buy chunks of pork, cut from the ribs, well cooked and meltingly tender under a crisp exterior from Rebelo's Portuguese take-out counter.

Steven and I were in the throes of newly found love. Steven was going to the University of Toronto at the time, working as a dishwasher on the weekend and living on cottage cheese and sliced ham. I thought I was a bit more sophisticated as far as food was concerned, having cooked in restaurants for five years, and had progressed as far as Ramen noodles. We thought we were truly in the know and would have small feasts of Brie cheese, pâté and French bread to prove it. It was time though, for something truly special, something unique, to celebrate our union. Lobster and Champagne was it! We would have a lobster feast on the roof of the house where I lived, gazing into the downtown skyscape of Toronto.

How do you buy a lobster and how do you cook it? Neither of us had cooked or eaten a whole lobster, ever, so it was with great fear and excitement that they were bought and cooked, although knowing myself as I do, I probably bluffed my way through it, imagining that I was shining with confidence. The most painstakingly careful hollandaise in the world was prepared and a bunch of asparagus was gingerly steamed. The champagne was chilled, and cheese, bread and strawberries laid out. We rushed our dinner up three floors to the roof where pillows, blankets and an electric lamp were set. We toasted each other and toasted the city. I don't remember eating except for scooping up the hollandaise with bread, and marveling at its texture and flavor. What I do remember is that it was one of the sweetest, most romantic and awe-filled nights of my life. We decided to sleep on the roof that night, and several hours into sleep were awakened by drops of rain.

This particular celebration has all the elements that make for a permanent celebration. There is anticipation, a bit of anxiety and excitement. There are feelings of discovery, contentment and an experience shared. There is, above all, good food, shared with good company.

You don't need a group for a feast or celebration. You could be all alone, tucked into the couch, well blanketed, content, and

feeling almost wicked because you are eating only for yourself. It is a grand moment of individual feasting and celebration. Two people often eat together, celebrating something special or simply indulging in foods that they really enjoy.

The book is divided into seasons that encompass what is good to eat, simply because it is in season. There are no recipes for fresh tomatoes in winter or oysters in summer. Why? Tomatoes just don't taste right and oysters are milky and spawning. Salmon and halibut have their season (although salmon is farmed in the winter), and so does corn. Consider halibut cheeks, asparagus and artichokes in the spring. Local prawns, zucchini, fresh basil and eggplant in summer. This is the time of year to cook lightly and simply, have barbecues and a multitude of salads. Corn, potatoes and apples in the fall. This is another transitional season, when you can begin to cook with a bolder stroke. Cabbage, oysters and beets in winter. Hot and steamy bowls of sausage with polenta, roast duck and mashed potatoes. Eating and cooking seasonally gives me a reason to celebrate each ingredient as it arrives, fresh, full of flavor and potential.

I must admit that I don't follow this to the letter. What you or I cook and eat depends on our mood, the people we are serving, our preferences, and how much effort we want to expend. Whatever you decide to do, enjoyment should be the motivating factor. Seasonal transitions are not dates on a calendar either—only you know when a season changes.

Consider daily, weekly and monthly events; they all have feast and celebration potential. Imagine passing on a feast through generations or to your friends who pass it on to their friends. You may go down in history as creator of the Feast for the First Aphid!

This is but a small sampling of my own feasting and celebrations. I hope they will become part of yours as well.

Spring

A Small Feast for Crocuses

Cheddar Cheese Soufflé

Peeled and Cooked Asparagus

A Good, Crusty Baguette

The Small Feast for Crocuses is more a state of mind than an actual event. When you can't stand the winter or wet spring anymore, it's time to break out the asparagus. I know that crocus and asparagus are not in season at the same time but I usually can't wait for the asparagus. I jump-start the season by peeling and cooking the best I can find, with a really runny cheese soufflé that serves as a sauce for the asparagus. The only other thing I offer with it is a good, crusty baguette. This is the only time of year I make a soufflé or peel asparagus.

Cheddar Cheese Soufflé

If a soft-centered soufflé is not to your taste, bake it for 35 minutes.

Serves 2-3

2 Tbsp.	unsalted butter	30 mL
2 Tbsp.	flour	30 mL
1 1/4 cups	milk	300 mL
1 tsp.	salt	5 mL
2 tsp.	Dijon mustard	10 mL
3	large egg yolks	3
1 1/2 cups	sharp, old, cheddar cheese, grated	360 mL
5	large egg whites	5

Preheat the oven to 400°F (200°C). Butter a 6-cup (1.5-L) soufflé dish and place in the fridge.

In a heavy pot, melt the butter over medium heat. Add the flour and stir for a minute without letting the flour brown. With a whisk, stir in the milk little by little. Stirring constantly, let the sauce come to a boil. Remove from the heat and beat in the salt, Dijon mustard and the egg yolks one at a time. Stir in the cheese till melted.

With an electric mixer or by hand, beat the egg whites to soft peaks. Whisk one-quarter of the egg whites into the cheese mixture, then fold in the remaining whites only until incorporated. Transfer to the soufflé dish and bake in the middle of the oven for 20-25 minutes. Serve immediately.

Peeled and Cooked Asparagus

I am not a thin asparagus person. I like big juicy spears you can really sink your teeth into.

Serves 2-3

2 lbs.	thick asparagus	900 g

Snap off the ends of the asparagus. Using a swivel-headed vegetable peeler, hold the tip of the asparagus towards you and peel the bottom of the spear, starting halfway down the stalk. Place the peeled spears facing in the same direction and loosely tie them into a bundle with string.

Bring a large pot of water to a boil and salt liberally. It should taste like seawater. Add the asparagus and cook until tender but still firm, 4-6 minutes. Remove the bundle, holding it over the pot for a few seconds to drain. Roll up in a clean kitchen towel to drain further. Unwrap, remove the strings and place on a heated plate. You can add butter if you wish, but I don't find it necessary with the soufflé. Serve with lemon wedges.

Easter Feast

Almost Seven-Hour Leg of Lamb

Creamed Spinach with Garam Masala

Rhubarb Cobbler

This is an easy dinner to prepare. The lamb, carrots, onion and potatoes cook together in the oven while the spinach cooks on top of the stove. Bake the rhubarb cobbler after the lamb comes out of the oven, so it will be warm for dessert. When I serve a big sit-down group, I like to have platters or bowls of all the dishes being served at each end of the table. This way everyone is served faster, which prevents anxiety while your guests are waiting to eat. Plus you don't have to heave heavy platters around the table and the food stays warmer.

If you want to serve an appetizer, a small portion of Clams with Bacon, Olives and Tomatoes, page 173, would stand up well before the lamb.

Almost Seven-Hour Leg of Lamb

The lamb braises for a long time in white wine and becomes so tender that you can eat it with a spoon.

Serves 8-10

6	medium onions, peeled and cut into quarters	6
6	medium carrots, peeled and cut into 3-inch (7.5-cm) pieces	6
20	cloves garlic, peeled and cut in half	20
6	bay leaves	6
6	small sprigs fresh thyme	6
1	leg of lamb, 7-8 lbs. (3.2-3.6 kg), trimmed of fat	1
	salt and pepper to taste	
6 cups	dry white wine	1.5 L
5 lbs.	russet potatoes, peeled and cut into 1 1/2-inch (4-cm) slices	2.3 kg
1	28-oz. (796-mL) can Italian plum tomatoes, coarsely chopped, with the juice	1

Preheat the oven to 425°F (220°C). Scatter the onions, carrots, garlic, bay leaves and thyme in a large roasting pan with a lid. Place the lamb on top of the vegetables and herbs and roast uncovered for 30 minutes. Season the lamb generously with salt and pepper and roast for 1 hour longer.

In a nonreactive pot, bring the wine to a boil. Pour over the lamb and cover with the lid. Turn the oven down to 325°F (165°C). Roast for about 4 hours longer, until the meat is very tender when pierced with a fork. Check the lamb after 3 hours; it may be ready at this point. Add the potatoes and tomatoes. Cover and return to the oven and roast for 1-1 1/2 hours longer, until the potatoes are tender.

Transfer the vegetables to two platters. Cover and keep warm. Remove the lamb to a cutting board. Pour the cooking juice into a bowl and skim the fat. Transfer to a pot and boil over high heat until slightly thickened. Season with salt and pepper. Carve the lamb into thick slices and place on the platters with the vegetables. Serve with the juice on the side.

Creamed Spinach with Garam Masala

This is excellent served with lamb. Garam masala is an East Indian blend of sweet spices, such as cinnamon, nutmeg and allspice. It is usually added at the last minute to cooked foods for an extra boost of flavor.

Serves 8

4 lbs.	fresh spinach, stemmed, washed and dried	1.8 kg
1 Tbsp.	unsalted butter	15 mL
4	cloves garlic, minced	4
4 Tbsp.	shallots, finely chopped	60 mL
2 cups	whipping cream	475 mL
1/2 tsp.	salt	2.5 mL
1 tsp.	fennel seeds	5 mL
1/2 tsp.	garam masala	2.5 mL
	pinch of cayenne pepper	

Coarsely chop the spinach and set aside. Melt the butter over medium heat in a large, heavy, preferably nonstick pot. Add the garlic and shallots and sauté until the shallots are translucent. Add the whipping cream and salt and bring to a simmer. Stir in the spinach by handfuls, adding more as it cooks down. Turn to low and cook, stirring frequently, until the spinach is extremely soft and the cream is almost absorbed, about 20 minutes. Heat a small frying pan over high heat. Add the fennel seeds and roast, shaking the pan, until the seeds turn one shade darker. Add to the spinach along with the garam masala and cayenne. Mix well.

Garam Masala

Make your own fresh garam masala and you will be amazed.

Makes 1/4 cup (60 mL)

2 Tbsp.	whole cumin seeds	30 mL
2 Tbsp.	whole coriander seeds	30 mL
2 tsp.	cardamom seeds (seeds removed from the pods)	10 mL
1	piece cinnamon stick, 3 inches (7.5 cm) long	1
3/4 tsp.	whole cloves	4 mL
1 Tbsp.	black peppercorns	15 mL
4	bay leaves	4

Heat a heavy frying pan over medium heat. Add the spices and roast, stirring constantly, until the spices are a few shades darker and are fragrant. Transfer to a plate and cool. Grind the spices to a powder in a spice mill or coffee grinder. Store in a covered jar.

Rhubarb Cobbler

How can such a simple dessert be so glorious? Oh richly browned, sweet and sour splendor!

Serves 8

3 cups	rhubarb, chopped into 1-inch (2.5-cm) pieces	720 mL
3/4 cup	brown sugar	180 mL
4 Tbsp.	butter, melted	60 mL
2	eggs, lightly beaten	2
1/2 cup	milk	120 mL
1 1/2 cups	flour	360 mL
2 tsp.	baking powder	10 mL
1 tsp.	vanilla	5 mL
1 cup	sugar	240 mL

Preheat the oven to 350°F (175°C). Generously butter a 9- by 13-inch (23- by 33-cm) baking dish.

In a medium-sized bowl, combine the rhubarb and brown sugar and set aside. In a large bowl, combine the remaining ingredients. Beat only until smooth.

Pour the batter into the buttered baking dish, then evenly spread the rhubarb mixture over the batter. Bake for 40 minutes. Serve warm, in a puddle of cream or with really good vanilla ice cream.

Feast for a Fool:
My Birthday Feast

My Birthday Ribs

Laotian Charred Tomato Sauce

Sticky Rice

Zebra Cake

Chocolate Milk

For years, my birthday feast has been ribs, a spicy Laotian charred tomato sauce, sticky rice, chocolate milk and Zebra Cake. A very adult bottle of nice, vintage port is opened later. The ribs, sticky rice and charred tomato sauce came from the incredible barbecues my Laotian friends have in the summer. The rest came later.

I am very dogmatic about foods that have to be picked up and eaten with your hands, such as ribs, corn or chicken wings: dishes requiring a fork cannot be served with them. These foods are pleasurable to eat with your hands and I don't see the point of putting down a rib, picking up a fork, and eating some macaroni salad. It's just too distracting. Steven and I have this argument every year during corn season. He will concede, but only once. For my birthday…well, *it's my party* and everyone eats with their hands.

My Birthday Ribs

*T*he initial
baking makes the
ribs tender, the sauce
and barbecuing or
broiling crisps them
up. I use a specific
saté sauce—Tia
Chieu Sa-té from
Huy Fong Foods. It
comes in an 8-oz.
(227-mL) plastic
bottle with a rooster
logo. You will find it
in stores that sell
Vietnamese products
and well-stocked
supermarkets. This
is a great sauce on
steaks too. The recipe
is easily doubled.

Serves 4

3 lbs.	pork side ribs	1.4 kg
	salt	
3 Tbsp.	ketchup	45 mL
3 Tbsp.	oyster sauce	45 mL
3 Tbsp.	saté sauce	45 mL
1/2 tsp.	Worcestershire sauce	2.5 mL

Preheat the oven to 300°F (150°C). Sprinkle the ribs lightly with salt and place in a single layer in baking pans. Pour in 1/2 inch (1.2 cm) water, cover tightly with aluminum foil and bake for 2 hours. Remove from the oven, uncover and cool.

Preheat the broiler or barbecue to medium. Mix the remaining ingredients together and brush on both sides of the ribs. Broil or grill the ribs until browned and crusty. Cut into single ribs before serving.

Laotian Charred Tomato Sauce

*L*aos has some of the most interesting sauces I have ever come across. These are thick sauces, used as a dip for meat, vegetables or the Lao staple, sticky rice. They sometimes contain fish or meat or can be vegetable-based like this one.

Makes 1 1/2 cups (360 mL)

1/2 lb.	cherry tomatoes	227 g
4	small shallots, unpeeled	4
6	cloves garlic, unpeeled	6
3	Thai chilies	3
1/2 tsp.	salt	2.5 mL
2 tsp.	fish sauce	10 mL
1/2 tsp.	sugar	2.5 mL
1 Tbsp.	freshly squeezed lime juice	15 mL

Heat a large, heavy, preferably cast-iron frying pan over medium-low heat. Place the tomatoes, shallots, garlic and chilies in separate piles in the frying pan. Cook the ingredients, turning each one, until the tomatoes and chilies have blackened in spots (the skins might split and this is fine) and the garlic and shallots are completely blackened. As they are done, remove the ingredients to a plate, keeping them separate. Cool.

Remove the blackened skins from the garlic and shallots. With a mortar and pestle or in a large bowl with a fork, mash the chilies and salt together. Add the garlic and shallots and mash to a rough paste. Add the tomatoes and mash until well incorporated. Stir in the fish sauce, sugar and lime juice. The sauce will keep for a week, covered and refrigerated.

Sticky Rice

*S*ticky rice is not
the rice used in
sushi. Sushi rice is
cooked Japanese rice
that has been tossed
and fanned with a
mixture of vinegar,
sugar and salt. This
gives it a lustrous
sheen and helps it to
stick together. I once
tried to assist a
couple in a Laotian
store looking for rice
for sushi. They were
holding a bag of
short grain
glutinous rice. I
explained that this
rice was not used for
sushi and they
dismissed me with a
bland smile. I had a
little chuckle,
thinking of how they
would be looking at
a nice pot of goo and
trying to figure out
what went wrong.

Serves 4-6

Sticky or glutinous rice is a variety of rice that is high in amylopectin, the component that makes rice sticky. It can be long or short grain. Long grain is used in Laos and northern Thailand as a daily rice. Viewed side by side with typical long grain rice, you will see that the glutinous rice is bright white, whereas the other is opaque. Short grain rice is used in other Asian cultures for desserts and stuffings. Anyone who is familiar with dim sum will know it as the filling, along with sausage, dried shrimp, egg yolk and chicken, of the lotus leaf wrap.

Two cups (475 mL) of raw rice will be enough for 4-6 people. Wash it several times in cool water and let it soak overnight. A special steaming apparatus that consists of an urn-shaped aluminum pot and a triangular, cone-shaped basket is used to cook the rice. Fill the bottom of the pot with a few inches of water and place the soaked rice in the basket. Cover with a lid and steam over high heat until the bottom rice is tender, about 5 minutes. Holding the basket by the top, deftly jerk it down, flipping the rice over. When the rice has finished steaming, transfer it to lidded baskets for serving.

Each diner takes a small handful of rice in the nondominant hand, pulls off a small clump, and with the other hand forms it into a tight ball. It is then used to convey food to the mouth. The ball has to be tight, especially when eating from communal dishes. It is a real no-no to leave grains of your rice in the dish. Stores selling Vietnamese, Thai or Laotian ingredients will carry the essentials for making sticky rice as well as beautiful clay mortars with wooden pestles for making the charred tomato sauce.

Zebra Cake

Serves 4-6

*O*ne year my dear friend Sjoerd made this cake with a Barbie doll sticking out of the cake part, a big, flouncy whipped cream skirt decorated with Smarties. It was a sight to behold!

Unfortunately, I cannot give you the recipe for Zebra Cake because it's on the back of the Christie Chocolate Wafers box and belongs to them. They call it Chocolate Wafer Log, a rather dull name I think when compared to the exciting Zebra Cake. It is thin chocolate wafers, sandwiched together and iced with whipped cream and left to sit overnight. Sitting overnight is what transforms it into a glorious deep brown and white striped cake. And if it's layered up in a round springform pan, it can actually fool people into thinking you spent days slaving over it.

But I can tell you why it is my birthday cake. Having cooked professionally for 20 years I always hear, "Oh, I could never cook for you!" People are naturally intimidated, although I appreciate it even when someone will make me a piece of toast! I started making this cake thinking that if anyone ever *wanted* to make my birthday cake, it would be a breeze for them. I have rarely had any offers, so I continue to make it, as well as my whole dinner, year after year.

The great thing about using chocolate wafers and whipping cream for a cake is it lends itself to construction, like bricks and mortar. I've made round cakes, dog cakes and snake cakes, to name a few, dyed the whipping cream in rainbow colors, decorated it with Easter eggs and KitKat bars. With Zebra Cake in your repertoire, there is never a dull moment!

Scalloped Halibut Cheeks

Halibut cheeks are one of the real thrills of halibut season. I like them better than any other part of the fish! You can also use halibut filets cut into 2- by 2- by 1-inch (5- by 5- by 2.5-cm) pieces for this dish.

To Make Soft White Breadcrumbs

To make soft white bread-crumbs, remove the crusts from a loaf of bread that is one or two days old and cut or tear it into 1-inch (2.5-cm) pieces. Place a handful into the workbowl of a food processor and pulse until large soft crumbs are formed. I have even done this in a coffee grinder. It works well for small quantities of crumbs.

Serves 4

1 1/2 lbs.	large halibut cheeks	680 g
	salt and pepper to taste	
1/2 cup	flour	120 mL
1 cup	whipping cream	240 mL
1 Tbsp.	fresh dill	15 mL
1	green onion, minced	1
2 Tbsp.	lemon juice	30 mL
1/4 tsp.	salt	1.2 mL
1 Tbsp.	butter, melted	15 mL
1 1/4 cups	soft white breadcrumbs	300 mL

Preheat the oven to 375°F (190°C).

Salt and pepper the halibut cheeks on both sides. Place the flour on a plate and dip the fish in the flour, coating both sides. Place the cheeks, keeping the smaller ones in the center, in a baking dish that will hold them snugly without overlapping.

Mix the whipping cream, dill, onion, lemon juice and 1/4 tsp. (1.2 mL) salt together and pour over the halibut cheeks. Place in the oven and bake for 15 minutes.

While the cheeks are baking, mix the melted butter and breadcrumbs together. When 15 minutes are up, remove the dish from the oven and sprinkle the buttered breadcrumbs over the halibut cheeks. Try to get the crumbs mostly on the fish, not the cream. Return to the oven and bake for 15 minutes longer, or until the flesh is opaque. If the crumbs are not quite browned, place the dish under the broiler until they turn a crunchy gold. Let the dish settle for a few minutes before serving.

Baked Salmon Steaks with Parsley, Vermouth and Cream

This dish has an out-of-fashion feel to it and, like many out-of-fashion foods, is extremely delicious. Perhaps in 10 years, we will all be feeling a little less than nouveau, remembering the gallons of sun-dried tomatoes and balsamic vinegar that we used indiscriminately. Enjoy with the timeless combination of tiny new potatoes and peas.

Serves 4

4	6-oz. (170-g) salmon steaks, 1 inch (2.5 cm) thick	4
1 cup	dry white vermouth	240 mL
1/4 cup	bottled or canned clam nectar	60 mL
2 Tbsp.	shallots, minced	30 mL
1	clove garlic, minced	1
1 cup	whipping cream	240 mL
1/4 cup	fresh parsley leaves	60 mL
	salt and pepper to taste	
1 Tbsp.	chives or the green tops of green onion, minced	15 mL

Preheat the oven to 350°F (175°C).

Place the salmon in a baking dish, without overlapping the steaks, and sprinkle with salt and pepper. Place in the oven and bake for 10-15 minutes, until the salmon is just opaque in the middle. Cover and keep warm.

While you are baking the salmon, make the sauce. In a small heavy saucepan, combine the vermouth, clam nectar, shallots and garlic. Bring to a boil and cook until the mixture is reduced to 3/4 cup (180 mL). Add the whipping cream and boil until the mixture is reduced to 1 1/2 cups (360 mL). Place half the mixture in a blender or food processor, add the parsley and purée. Stir into the remaining mixture, then press through a sieve. Return to the pot and boil until the mixture coats a spoon, 2-3 minutes. Season with salt and pepper.

Add pan juices from the salmon and the chives or green onion to the sauce. Place the salmon on heated plates or a platter, pour the sauce around the steaks and serve immediately.

Fish and Seafood

Salmon "Carpaccio" with Mushroom Salad and Shaved Parmesan

Serve as an elegant first course or as part of a tapas-style dinner.

Serves 4

3/4 lb.	fresh, boneless salmon filet	340 g
2 Tbsp.	lemon juice	30 mL
1/2 tsp.	salt	2.5 mL
1	clove garlic, cut in half	1
1/2 cup	olive oil	120 mL
1/2 lb.	firm white mushrooms	227 g
1/4 cup	fresh basil leaves	60 mL
1 Tbsp.	fresh parsley, coarsely chopped	15 mL
	freshly ground black pepper	
	a large chunk of Parmesan or grana	
	padano cheese	

Slice the salmon into micro-thin slices and lay on a large platter or individual plates closely together but without overlapping. Cover with plastic wrap and refrigerate.

Place the lemon juice, salt and garlic in a small bowl and beat well with a fork. Slowly beat in the olive oil. Set aside.

Thinly slice the mushrooms. Tear the basil leaves into small pieces and add half the basil to the mushrooms, along with the chopped parsley. Cover and refrigerate.

Just before serving, remove the salmon from the fridge. Beat the dressing well to recombine and drizzle half of it over the salmon. Grind pepper to taste over the salmon. Combine the remaining dressing with the mushrooms and mix well. Place the mushroom salad in the center of the platter or plates of salmon. With a vegetable peeler, shave long shreds of cheese over the salmon and mushrooms. Scatter the remaining half of the basil leaves over the whole dish and serve immediately.

◆ 19 ◆

Salmon Marinated in Lapsang Souchong Tea

Lapsang Souchong is a delicious, smoked Chinese tea. I have loved its flavor since my teens, and became interested again in its potential when I had an especially good one at a Vancouver institution called "T" that deals exclusively in quality teas. The charming proprietors sent me home with a bag and this is what I came up with. This salmon is sweet, smoky and very delicious.

Serves 6 as an appetizer, 2-3 as a main course

1 tsp.	salt	5 mL
2 tsp.	sugar	10 mL
1 lb.	boneless, skinless salmon filet	454 g
1/4 cup	Lapsang Souchong tea	60 mL
1 Tbsp.	vegetable oil	15 mL

Mix the salt and sugar together and sprinkle both sides of the filet. Sprinkle both sides of the filet with the tea, pressing it gently onto the fish. Cover and refrigerate overnight.

Scrape the tea from the salmon. In a heavy, nonstick frying pan, heat the vegetable oil over medium-low heat. Place the salmon filet in the pan and cook until the outside is brown and crispy, about 3-4 minutes on each side. Remove from the heat and let sit for a minute before serving.

Rainbow Trout with Tarragon and Lime

You can use salmon filets or steaks in place of the trout.

Serves 4

2 Tbsp.	lime juice	30 mL
1/2 tsp.	salt	2.5 mL
1 Tbsp.	fresh tarragon, finely chopped	15 mL
2	green onions, thinly sliced	2
2 Tbsp.	olive oil	30 mL
4	whole, boned rainbow trout, about 8 oz. (227 g) each	4
4 Tbsp.	fine dry breadcrumbs	60 mL
	lime wedges for garnishing	

Combine the lime, salt, tarragon, green onion and olive oil in a small bowl.

Preheat the broiler to high. Lightly oil a baking pan. Spread the trout open and place skin side up on the pan. Spoon half the marinade over the fish and sprinkle with half the breadcrumbs.

Broil 4 inches (10 cm) from the heat for 3-4 minutes. Turn the trout over and spoon the remaining marinade and breadcrumbs over the fish. Broil for another 3-4 minutes, until the fish is just opaque all the way through. Serve on heated plates.

Scallop, Leek and Potato Chowder

Good on a chilly day served with hot cornbread.

Serves 4

1 lb.	red potatoes, cooked and cooled	454 g
1 Tbsp.	unsalted butter	15 mL
4	slices bacon, finely chopped	4
3	leeks, white and light green part only, thinly sliced (see A Bit About Leeks, page 191)	3
1	jalapeño pepper, finely chopped	1
1/2 cup	sweet red pepper, finely diced	120 mL
1/2 cup	celery, finely diced	120 mL
2 1/2 cups	canned or bottled clam nectar	600 mL
	salt and pepper to taste	
1 lb.	sea scallops, foot removed, cut in half lengthwise	454 g
1/2 cup	whipping cream or milk	120 mL
2 Tbsp.	fresh parsley, finely chopped	30 mL

Dice the cooked potatoes into 1/2-inch (1.2-cm) pieces and set aside.

In a large pot, melt the butter over medium heat. Add the bacon and sauté until the bacon starts to color. Add the leeks, peppers and celery and sauté until the vegetables are soft but not brown, 4-5 minutes. Add the clam nectar and potatoes. Bring to a boil and simmer for 10 minutes. Season with salt and pepper. Add the scallops, cream or milk and parsley. Cook, stirring occasionally, until the scallops are firm, 2-3 minutes. Serve in heated bowls.

Spaghettini with Spicy Scallops

For days when you need a dish that is fast, simple and elegant.

Serves 4

6 Tbsp.	olive oil	90 mL
6	cloves garlic, minced	6
1/2 tsp.	crushed chili flakes	2.5 mL
1 cup	fresh or canned plum tomatoes, finely chopped	240 mL
2 Tbsp.	fresh parsley, coarsely chopped	30 mL
1 lb.	sea scallops, foot removed, cut into quarters	454 g
	salt and pepper to taste	
1 lb.	spaghettini	454 g

Bring a large pot of water to a boil. While waiting for it to boil, prepare the sauce. Heat the olive oil in a large frying pan over medium heat. Add the garlic and chili flakes and cook until the garlic just starts to turn golden. Add the tomatoes and bring to a boil. Add the parsley and scallops, stir and remove from the heat. Season with salt and pepper.

Add the spaghettini to the boiling water and salt liberally. It should taste like seawater. Cook, stirring the pasta occasionally, until it is tender but still firm to the bite. Drain and return the pasta to the pot. Stir in the scallop mixture over low heat until heated through. Transfer to heated bowls and serve immediately.

Pickled Prawns

These make a great nibbler, an interesting cocktail or a great addition to a tossed salad. If you want to get really fancy, garnish the rim of a Bloody Caesar with them.

Makes about 45 prawns

1 cup	white wine vinegar	240 mL
4	thin slices fresh ginger	4
4 Tbsp.	coriander seeds	60 mL
1 Tbsp.	mustard seeds	15 mL
1 Tbsp.	fennel seeds	15 mL
1 tsp.	whole allspice berries	5 mL
1	2-inch (5-cm) piece cinnamon stick	1
8	whole cloves	8
1 tsp.	whole black peppercorns	5 mL
1 tsp.	salt	5 mL
2 Tbsp.	sugar	30 mL
2 lbs.	large prawns, approximately 45-50, peeled and deveined	900 g
1	small red onion, cut into thin rings	1
2	small lemons, thinly sliced and seeded	2
5	garlic cloves, thickly sliced lengthwise	5
4	dried chilies, broken in half	4
4	bay leaves	4
1 cup	olive oil	240 mL

In a noncorrodible pot, combine the vinegar, ginger, coriander, mustard, fennel, allspice, cinnamon, cloves, peppercorns, salt and sugar. Bring to a boil and simmer for 10 minutes. Remove from the heat and let the liquid cool.

Bring a large pot of water to a boil. Add the prawns and stir until they turn pink, 2-3 minutes. Drain and cool.

Layer the prawns in a narrow 6-cup (1.5-L) jar with the onion, lemon, garlic, chilies and bay leaves. Beat the olive oil into the pickling liquid and pour over the prawns. Cover and refrigerate for 2 days, shaking the jar every day. The prawns are now ready to eat and will keep for 5 days, refrigerated.

Chicken Steamed with Ginger and Sherry

This dish is well worth the price of a steamer and has the sort of innocent, pure flavors that make me wish it would never stop. Serve it with steamed rice and Wok-Seared Bean Sprouts, page 43.

Steamers and Steaming

Large, lightweight aluminum steamers can be purchased in Asian grocery stores and well-stocked cookware shops. They usually have two steamer baskets that fit snugly over the pot with a tight-fitting lid. A whole meal or all the vegetables for, say, Christmas dinner can be cooked in separate bowls with a minimum of fuss and bother. Steaming is a very fast and gentle method of cooking. Most people are familiar with the great taste of steamed vegetables but may not be aware that the same technique produces equally delicious fish and meat. If fat is a concern to you, marinating and steaming fish and meat is a way to delicious, healthful cooking.

Serves 4

2	green onions	2
6	1/4 -inch (.6-cm) slices fresh ginger	6
2 tsp.	salt	10 mL
1/4 cup	medium dry sherry or Chinese cooking wine	60 mL
1	chicken, approximately 2 1/2 lbs. (1.1 kg)	1
1	4-inch (10-cm) piece peeled ginger, sliced	1
2	green onions, chopped	2
1/4 tsp.	salt	1.2 mL
2 Tbsp.	vegetable oil	30 mL

With the flat of a knife, lightly smash the green onions and sliced ginger. Place in a bowl large enough to hold the chicken and comfortably fit in the steamer. Add the 2 tsp. (10 mL) salt and sherry or wine and mix well. Place the chicken in the bowl, rolling it around in the marinade, and place a few spoonfuls inside the chicken. Let stand for half an hour. Bring 4 inches (10 cm) of water to a boil in the bottom of the steamer. Place the chicken in the steamer basket, cover with the lid and place on top of the boiling water. Steam for 40 minutes without removing the lid. Turn off the heat and let stand for 15 minutes.

While the chicken is steaming, prepare the ginger sauce. Place the second amount of ginger, chopped green onion, 1/4 tsp. (1.2 mL) salt and oil in a blender or food processor. Pulse until the ingredients are finely chopped but still have some texture. Don't purée it. Scrape into a bowl.

Remove the chicken from the steamer. Either carve the chicken or chop it as I do into sections, using a heavy knife or cleaver. Place on a heated platter and pour some of the steaming juices over it. If you don't care about a fancy presentation, just put it back in the bowl you steamed it in. Serve immediately with the ginger sauce on the side. Strain and save the delicious steaming juices. I like to heat them with cooked orzo and a bit of Parmesan cheese for a quick soupy pasta. If there is any chicken left over, I dice it and add it too.

Whole Spiced Chicken Baked in Parchment Paper

Serve this spicy, luscious chicken with Corn and Basmati Rice Pilaf, page 97. You can bake the chicken in heavy-duty aluminum foil instead of parchment paper.

Serves 4-6

1	whole chicken, about 3 lbs. (1.4 kg)	1

For the marinade:

1	1-inch (2.5-cm) piece of fresh ginger, peeled and chopped	1
2	cloves garlic, peeled and chopped	2
6 Tbsp.	yogurt	90 mL
1/2 tsp.	turmeric	2.5 mL
1 tsp.	salt	5 mL
1/4 tsp.	cayenne pepper	1.2 mL

For the spice paste:

1	medium onion, chopped	1
4	cloves garlic, peeled and chopped	4
1	walnut-sized piece of ginger, peeled and chopped	1
2 tsp.	ground cumin seeds	10 mL
2 tsp.	ground coriander seeds	10 mL
1/2 tsp.	turmeric	2.5 mL
1 Tbsp.	paprika	15 mL
1/4 tsp.	cayenne pepper	1.2 mL
1 tsp.	salt	5 mL
1/2 tsp.	ground black pepper	2.5 mL
1/2 tsp.	garam masala (see page 10)	2.5 mL
4 Tbsp.	vegetable oil	60 mL
2 Tbsp.	lemon juice	30 mL

Remove the skin and fat from the chicken. Place all the marinade ingredients in the work bowl of a food processor or blender and process until a fine paste is formed. Rub the chicken inside and out with the paste. Cover and refrigerate for 2 hours.

While the chicken is marinating, make the spice paste. Combine the onion, garlic and ginger in the work bowl of a blender or food processor. Purée until a fine paste is formed. Add all the remaining ingredients except the oil and lemon juice and blend until combined.

Heat the oil in a nonstick pan over medium-high heat. Add the spice paste and fry, stirring frequently, until the paste is dry and light brown. Remove from the heat and add the lemon juice. Let cool.

Preheat the oven to 350°F (175°C). Lay out two pieces of parchment paper that are large enough to enclose the chicken comfortably. Place one on top of the other. Rub the chicken inside and out with the spice paste. Place the chicken on the parchment paper. Bring the ends of the parchment paper over the chicken and fold down to form a tight seal. Fold the remaining ends tightly.

Place in the oven and bake for 2 hours. An instant-read thermometer is extremely useful to check if the chicken is done. Push the thermometer through the parchment into the thickest part of the thigh. It should read 180°F (85°C). Remove from the oven and let the chicken sit for 10 minutes. You may serve the chicken at the table, opening up the parchment to enjoy the first delicious rush of fragrance, or cut it up in the kitchen. Serve with the juices.

Smoked Chicken, Melon and Watercress Salad

Look for a naturally smoked chicken instead of that nasty, hamlike stuff that masquerades as smoked chicken. You can use smoked turkey, duck or a roasted chicken instead of a smoked chicken, and any combination of melons you prefer.

Serves 4

1 Tbsp.	shallots, finely minced	15 mL
1/4 tsp.	salt	1.2 mL
1/2 tsp.	sugar	2.5 mL
1 Tbsp.	cider or white wine vinegar	15 mL
1 tsp.	Dijon mustard	5 mL
1/4 cup	vegetable oil	60 mL
1 tsp.	fresh tarragon, chopped	5 mL
1	bunch watercress, coarse stems removed	1
3 cups	boneless smoked chicken, cut into bite-sized pieces	720 mL
1 cup	honeydew melon, cut into 1/2-inch (1.2-cm) cubes	240 mL
1 cup	cantaloupe, cut into 1/2-inch (1.2-cm) cubes	240 mL

In a small bowl, whisk the shallots, salt, sugar, vinegar and mustard together. Slowly beat in the oil. Stir in the tarragon.

In a serving bowl, combine the watercress, chicken, melon and cantaloupe. Pour the dressing over the salad and toss well.

Chicken Breasts with Far Eastern Spices

Serve this with a cucumber, tomato and onion salad sprinkled with fresh mint or cilantro, and extra yogurt on the side. The chicken may be grilled or pan-roasted if you prefer.

Serves 4-6

6	6-oz. (170-g) boneless, skinless chicken breast halves	6
1/4 cup	freshly squeezed lemon juice	60 mL
1/2 tsp.	salt	2.5 mL
4 Tbsp.	yogurt	60 mL
4 tsp.	ground coriander	20 mL
2 tsp.	ground cumin	10 mL
1 tsp.	turmeric	5 mL
1 tsp.	bright red paprika	5 mL
1/2 tsp.	ground ginger	1.2 mL
	pinch of cayenne pepper	
4	cloves garlic, minced	4
1/4 cup	green onion, thinly sliced	60 mL
1 Tbsp.	vegetable oil	15 mL

Combine the chicken breasts, lemon juice and salt in a bowl and mix well. Let stand for 30 minutes. Mix the yogurt, coriander, cumin, turmeric, paprika, ginger, cayenne pepper, garlic, green onion and oil together. Pour over the chicken and stir well to coat. Cover and refrigerate 2 hours or up to overnight.

Preheat the broiler to high. Place the chicken on a baking pan and broil 4 inches (10 cm) away from the heat for 4-6 minutes, until lightly browned. Turn the chicken over and broil for 2-3 minutes, until the chicken is cooked through.

Garlicky Chicken with Feta and Oregano

Serve this chicken with sautéed or grilled peppers and Orzo with Lemon and Herbs, page 47.

Serves 4

1/2 cup	yogurt	120 mL
1	green onion, thinly sliced	1
1 tsp.	fresh parsley, finely chopped	5 mL
4	cloves garlic, minced	4
1/2 tsp.	dried oregano	2.5 mL
1/3 tsp.	salt	1.7 mL
1/4 tsp.	pepper	1.2 mL
4	6-oz. (170-g) boneless, skinless chicken breast halves	4
1/2 cup	crumbled feta cheese	120 mL

Combine the yogurt, green onion, parsley, garlic, oregano, salt and pepper in a medium-sized bowl. Add the chicken breasts and mix well to coat with the marinade. Refrigerate, covered, for at least 30 minutes or up to 1 day.

Preheat the broiler to high. Place the chicken on a baking pan and broil 4 inches (10 cm) away from the heat for 4-6 minutes, until lightly browned. Turn the chicken over and sprinkle with the feta cheese. Broil for 2-3 minutes, until the chicken is cooked through and the cheese is speckled with brown. Serve on heated plates.

Flat Roasted Chicken with Sweet Carrots, Prosciutto and Olives

Finding a bunch of tender, glowing carrots was the inspiration for this recipe. The prosciutto and olives temper their sweetness and the wine adds the needed sour edge. A beautiful combination of flavors.

Serves 4

1	chicken, 3 1/2-4 lbs. (1.6-1.8 kg)	1
	salt and pepper	
1/2 cup	prosciutto, diced into 1/4-inch (.6-cm) cubes	120 mL
1/3 cup	shallots, minced	80 mL
2 cups	carrots, peeled and cut into 1/2-inch (1.2-cm) cubes	475 mL
2	cloves garlic, minced	2
1/2 cup	whole green olives, unpitted	120 mL
1/2 cup	white wine	120 mL
	salt and pepper to taste	

Preheat the oven to 350°F (175°C).

With a sharp heavy knife, split the chicken down the backbone and open it up. Turn it breast side up and flatten with the palm of your hand. Cut a slit in the skin at the bottom of the breast and slip the "ankles" of the chicken through the slit. Sprinkle liberally with salt and pepper. Transfer the chicken, breast side down, to a lightly oiled roasting pan. Bake for 45 minutes. While the chicken is baking, prepare and combine the prosciutto, shallots, carrots, garlic and olives.

Remove the chicken from the oven and transfer to a plate. Remove any accumulated fat from the roasting pan. Scatter the carrot mixture evenly in the roasting pan and add the white wine. Place the chicken in the pan skin side up. Bake for 45 minutes longer.

Remove the chicken from the pan. Either carve the chicken or transfer it whole to a heated platter. Pour the carrot mixture over the chicken and serve.

Leg of Lamb with Ginger and Sweet and Hot Spices

The lamb is also delicious cooked on the barbecue. If you want to barbecue it, place the lamb on a grill preheated to high and sear it for 5-8 minutes on each side. Turn the heat to low and cook for 10-15 minutes on each side for medium-rare. Brush frequently with the marinade while the lamb is cooking. Remove from the barbecue and let rest 10 minutes before carving across the grain.

Serves 6

1	butterflied leg of lamb, 3-4 lbs. (1.4-1.8 kg)	1
1	medium-sized onion, chopped	1
1	piece of fresh ginger, 3 inches (7.5 cm) long, peeled and chopped	1
6	cloves garlic, chopped	6
1/3 cup	lemon juice	80 mL
1 Tbsp.	ground coriander seeds	15 mL
1 tsp.	ground cumin	5 mL
1 tsp.	garam masala (see page 10)	5 mL
1 tsp.	turmeric	5 mL
1/4 tsp.	ground nutmeg	1.2 mL
1/4 tsp.	ground cinnamon	1.2 mL
1/4 tsp.	ground cloves	1.2 mL
1/2 cup	vegetable oil	120 mL
2 tsp.	salt	10 mL
1/2 tsp.	ground black pepper	2.5 mL
1/2 tsp.	cayenne pepper	2.5 mL

Trim the fat from the lamb leg. Prick the leg with the point of a small knife about 20 times on both sides.

Blend the chopped onion, ginger, garlic and lemon juice to a fine purée in the work bowl of a blender or food processor. Place in a container large enough to hold the lamb leg and add all the remaining ingredients except the lamb. Mix well.

Place the lamb in the container with the spice mixture and rub it thoroughly into both sides of the leg. Cover and refrigerate overnight.

Preheat the oven to 400°F (200°C). Place the lamb on a baking sheet and bake for 45 minutes for medium-rare (see How Do I Know When It's Done?, page 119). Heat the broiler and broil the lamb on both sides until crusty and brown. Let the lamb rest 10 minutes before carving across the grain.

Lamb Steaks with Garlic, Cumin and Black Pepper

I love the heady combination of cumin and garlic with lamb. Pair it with Lovely Lemon Potatoes, page 140, for a Mediterranean feast!

Serves 4

4	cloves garlic, minced	4
1/2 tsp.	salt	2.5 mL
1/2 tsp.	ground cumin seeds	2.5 mL
	pinch of cayenne pepper	
1/2 tsp.	coarsely ground black pepper	2.5 mL
1 Tbsp.	olive oil	15 mL
4	8-oz. (227-g) lamb leg steaks, about 1 inch (2.5 cm) thick	4

In a small bowl, combine the garlic, salt, cumin, cayenne and black pepper. Mash to a paste with the back of a spoon. Add the olive oil and mix well.

Place the steaks in a bowl and add the olive oil mixture. Toss well with your hands to evenly coat the steaks with the mixture.

Heat a large, heavy frying pan over medium-high heat. Add a dribble of vegetable oil and spread it over the bottom with a paper towel. Place the steaks in the pan and cook for 3-4 minutes, until well browned. (Turn on your stove fan. Seared black pepper will make you cough!) Turn the steaks over and cook for 3 more minutes for medium-rare. If you want them done more than medium-rare, reduce the heat to medium-low and cook until done to your liking. Serve on heated plates.

Whole Pot-roasted Lamb Shoulder with Macaroni

A luscious dish with an earthy "cooked all day" taste. If you want to serve a crowd, you can double the sauce ingredients and the amount of pasta used. Cut the lamb into small pieces and toss with the pasta and sauce.

Serves 8

1	whole lamb shoulder, bone in, about 5-6 lbs. (2.3-2.7 kg)	1
2 Tbsp.	vegetable oil	30 mL
2 cups	onion, finely diced	475 mL
4	cloves garlic, minced	4
2 cups	red wine	475 mL
4 cups	drained, canned plum tomatoes, puréed	950 mL
2	3-inch (7.5-cm) sticks cinnamon	2
4	whole cloves	4
1	bay leaf	1
1 tsp.	salt	5 mL
1 tsp.	sugar	5 mL
	salt and pepper to taste	
1 lb.	tubular pasta, such as penne, macaroni or ziti	454 g
1 cup	grated Romano cheese	240 mL

Preheat the oven to 300°F (150°C). Trim the lamb shoulder of excess fat. In a large ovenproof pot, heat the oil over medium heat. Add the lamb shoulder and brown on all sides. Remove from the pot. Add the onion and garlic to the pot and cook until the onion is translucent. Add the red wine and tomatoes, cinnamon, cloves, bay leaf, salt and sugar. Bring to a boil.

Place the lamb, meat side down, in the pot and cover tightly with a lid or aluminum foil. Bake for 1 1/2 hours. Turn the meat over and bake for another 1 1/2 hours. Remove the lamb from the pot, cover and keep warm.

Skim the fat from the tomato sauce left in the pot. Boil over high heat, stirring occasionally, until the sauce thickens slightly. Taste and adjust the seasoning.

Bring a large pot of water to a boil. Salt liberally. It should taste like seawater. Add the pasta and cook until it is just tender to the tooth. Drain and place back in the pot. Add half the tomato sauce and the Romano cheese. Transfer to

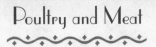

a large casserole dish. Cut the lamb into slices and chunks and place on top of the pasta. Cover with the remaining tomato sauce. Cover the dish with a lid or aluminum foil and bake for 15 minutes until piping hot. Remove the cover and serve from the pot.

My Meatloaf

Everybody and everybody's mother has a meatloaf recipe that is the best meatloaf (or sometimes the worst) in the entire world. Well, the one I make, is of course, the best in the entire world. So there!

Serves 6-8

1 cup	milk	240 mL
2 1/2 cups	1/2-inch (1.2-cm) cubes of good white bread, crust removed	600 mL
1 1/2 lbs.	lean ground beef	680 g
1 1/2 lbs.	ground pork	680 g
3/4 cup	onion, finely diced	180 mL
4 Tbsp.	fresh parsley, finely chopped	60 mL
1/2 tsp.	salt	2.5 mL
1/2 tsp.	ground black pepper	2.5 mL
1 cup	freshly grated Parmesan cheese	240 mL
6 oz.	prosciutto, finely diced	170 g
3	eggs	3

Preheat the oven to 350°F (175°C). Heat the milk in a small saucepan until it is quite hot. Add the bread cubes, stir a few times and remove from the heat to cool.

In a large bowl, combine the beef, pork, onion, parsley, salt, pepper and Parmesan cheese.

Place the prosciutto in the work bowl of a food processor and pulse until finely chopped. Add the cooled bread mixture and the eggs and pulse until the mixture is homogeneous. If you don't have a food processor, mix with a whisk until well combined. Add to the meat.

Mix with your hands until everything is well combined. Pack into a 10- by 5-inch (25- by 13-cm) loaf pan. Bake for 1 1/2 hours. Let rest for 10 minutes before serving.

Seafood and Pork Mu Shu with Hoisin Sauce and Napa Cabbage Wrap

This may look long and complicated, but once you have all the ingredients assembled and marinated, the cooking goes quickly. All the ingredients can be found at Asian grocery stores or well-stocked supermarkets.

Serves 4

The pork marinade:

1 tsp.	soy sauce	5 mL
1/4 tsp.	sugar	1.2 mL
1 tsp.	Chinese cooking wine	5 mL
1/2 tsp.	cornstarch	2.5 mL
1/8 tsp.	five spice powder	.5 mL
1/4 lb.	lean pork loin, julienned	113 g

The scallop and prawn marinade:

2 tsp.	cornstarch	10 mL
2 tsp.	Chinese cooking wine	10 mL
1/2 tsp.	sugar	2.5 mL
1/4 tsp.	salt	1.2 mL
1/2 tsp.	soy sauce	2.5 mL
1/8 tsp.	five spice powder	.5 mL
1/4 lb.	scallops	113 g
1/4 lb.	small prawns, peeled	113 g

To make the dish:

4	eggs	4
1/8 tsp.	salt	.5 mL
1 tsp.	soy sauce	5 mL
4	dried cloud ear mushrooms, soaked in hot water until soft	4
	napa or sui choi cabbage leaves	
	hoisin sauce	
1/2 cup	roasted peanuts, chopped	120 mL
5 Tbsp.	vegetable oil	75 mL
4	green onions, cut into 1-inch (2.5-cm) lengths	4
2 Tbsp.	Chinese cooking wine	30 mL
1 Tbsp.	soy sauce	15 mL

Combine all the pork marinade ingredients except the pork in a bowl. Add the julienned pork and stir well to coat. Cover and refrigerate for at least 1 hour or up to overnight. Repeat the process for the scallops and prawns.

Beat the eggs, salt and soy sauce together. Set aside. Remove the small, nubby stems from the cloud ear mushrooms and discard. Finely julienne the mushrooms and set aside.

Arrange the cabbage leaves, a small bowl of hoisin sauce and a small bowl of peanuts on a platter.

Heat a wok or large frying pan over high heat. Swirl 2 Tbsp. (30 mL) of the oil around the pan. Add the egg mixture and wait several seconds for the egg to set on the bottom. Push the cooked portion to the side of the pan, letting the loose egg flow to the bottom of the pan. Continue pushing the cooked egg to the side of the pan until the eggs are loosely set. Remove from the pan and break the egg into small pieces.

Quickly clean the wok and place back on high heat. Swirl 1 Tbsp. (15 mL) of the oil around the pan. Add the green onions and mushrooms and stir-fry for a few seconds. Add 1 Tbsp. (15 mL) of the cooking wine. Stir-fry for a few seconds longer. Add to the eggs.

Quickly clean the wok and place back on high heat. Swirl the remaining 2 Tbsp. (30 mL) oil into the pan. Add the pork, scallops and prawns and stir-fry until the meat is 90 percent done. Add the eggs and vegetables and season with the soy sauce and the remaining cooking wine. Stir-fry until everything is piping hot. Transfer to a hot serving platter.

To eat, spread a leaf of cabbage with a dab of hoisin sauce. Place some of the mu shu on top and sprinkle with the peanuts. Roll up and eat.

Frittata in Six Layers

A twist on the traditional frittata, the ingredients are cooked in six separate layers and assembled into a cake. The whole kit 'n' kaboodle is layered up, weighted and served at room temperature. Good on a buffet, as a warm-weather main course or as part of an antipasto spread. You can change the fillings as you see fit.

Serves 4-6

12	large eggs	12
6 Tbsp.	water	90 mL
	salt and pepper to taste	
3 Tbsp.	prosciutto, finely chopped	45 mL
2 Tbsp.	pesto	30 mL
3 Tbsp.	roasted sweet red peppers , coarsely chopped (see Roasting Peppers, page 98)	45 mL
3 Tbsp.	pitted black olives, coarsely chopped	45 mL
3 Tbsp.	freshly grated Parmesan cheese	45 mL
3 Tbsp.	oil-packed or rehydrated sun-dried tomatoes, finely chopped	45 mL
2 Tbsp.	olive oil	30 mL

Line a 6- to 7-inch (15- to 17.5-cm) straight-sided soufflé-type dish with plastic wrap, leaving a few inches (6 cm) of overhang all around.

Beat two eggs and 1 Tbsp. (15 mL) of the water into each of six small bowls. Season with salt and pepper. Add the prosciutto to one bowl, pesto to another, red peppers to the next, and so on with the black olives, Parmesan cheese and sun-dried tomatoes.

Heat a 6- to 7-inch (15- to 17.5-cm) nonstick frying pan over high heat. Add 1 tsp. (5 mL) of the olive oil. Starting with the prosciutto mixture, cook it into an omelette, using whatever your preferred method is, until barely set. Place in the casserole. Continue cooking the remaining omelettes, stacking them one on top of the other. Let cool.

Fold the plastic wrap over the top and place a small plate directly on top of the stacked omelettes. Weight down with a can or bottle filled with water and refrigerate for 2-3 hours. Remove from the refrigerator 1/2 hour before serving. Open up the plastic wrap and flip the dish upside down onto a serving plate. Remove the plastic wrap. Cut into wedges and serve.

Spinach Salad with Roasted Sweet Potatoes, Apples and Bacon Vinaigrette

Serve with pork and chicken dishes or with a good bread and a wedge of creamy blue cheese.

Serves 4-6

2	large sweet potatoes, peeled and cut into 1/2-inch (1.2-cm) cubes	2
2 Tbsp.	vegetable oil	30 mL
2 tsp.	fresh thyme leaves, chopped	10 mL
	salt and pepper to taste	
2	large Granny Smith apples, peeled and cut into 1/2-inch (1.2-cm) cubes	2
1/2 lb.	good-quality slab bacon, cut into 1/4-inch (.6-cm) dice	227 g
	vegetable oil	
3 Tbsp.	apple cider vinegar	45 mL
1 Tbsp.	honey	15 mL
3	green onions, thinly sliced	3
	salt and pepper to taste	
1 1/2 lb.	fresh spinach, stems removed, washed and dried	680 g

Preheat the oven to 400°F (200°C). Toss the sweet potatoes with the oil, thyme, and salt and pepper. Spread out in a baking dish in a single layer, cover tightly with aluminum foil and bake for 10 minutes. Remove the foil and push the potatoes to one side. Place the apples on the other side and bake for 10-15 minutes longer, until the potatoes are tender.

In a large frying pan over low heat, fry the bacon until crisp. Drain the fat into a heatproof measuring cup and add vegetable oil to make 1/2 cup (120 mL). Add the vinegar, honey and green onion to the bacon and bring to a simmer. Whisk in the oil and bacon fat. Season with salt and pepper.

Combine the spinach, sweet potatoes and apples in a serving bowl. Pour the hot vinaigrette over the salad and toss well.

Spinach Salad with Basil and Buttermilk Dressing

A traditional style of spinach salad with a delicious new dressing.

Serves 4-6

2 lbs.	fresh spinach, stems removed, washed and dried	900 g
1 recipe	Basil and Buttermilk Dressing	1 recipe
1/2 lb.	bacon, cooked until crisp, drained and crumbled	227 g
1	red onion, thinly sliced into rings	1
1/2 lb.	cultivated mushrooms, thinly sliced	227 g
2	hard-cooked eggs, finely chopped	2
2	medium-sized ripe tomatoes, cut into 8 wedges each	2
1/2 cup	toasted sesame seeds	120 mL

Tear the spinach into bite-sized pieces and transfer to a large bowl. Add enough of the dressing to coat the spinach leaves and toss well. Scatter the remaining ingredients over the salad and drizzle with enough dressing to coat all the ingredients well.

Basil and Buttermilk Dressing

This dressing is good on sliced tomatoes and cucumbers too.

Makes about 2 cups (475 mL)

2 cups	fresh basil leaves, lightly packed	475 mL
3/4 cup	buttermilk	180 mL
2	green onions, thinly sliced	2
3/4 tsp.	salt	4 mL
3/4 cup	mayonnaise	180 mL
1/2 tsp.	pepper	2.5 mL
1 Tbsp.	cider or white wine vinegar	15 mL

Combine the basil leaves, buttermilk, green onion and salt in a blender or food processor. Blend until smooth. Transfer to a bowl and stir in the remaining ingredients. Let stand for 30 minutes to blend the flavors.

French Food

This salad is a Vietnamese interpretation of what I suppose is a French potato salad. When we worked at the David Wood Food Shop in Toronto, Thao, a co-worker of my husband, used to make it for the deli. When we asked her what the salad was called she said, "French Food," and the name has stuck to it ever since. You can cook the carrots and beets in water instead of roasting them, but the flavor won't be as sweet.

Serves 4-6

1 lb.	new potatoes, about 4	454 g
6 oz.	baby beets, about 10 walnut-sized beets	170 g
6 oz.	small carrots, about 3	170 g
2	eggs, hard-cooked	2
1/2 cup	celery hearts, thinly sliced	120 mL
2	green onions, thinly sliced	2
3 Tbsp.	fresh cilantro, coarsely chopped	45 mL
3 Tbsp.	fresh mint leaves, coarsely chopped	45 mL
1 Tbsp.	vegetable oil	15 mL
2	cloves garlic, minced	2
2 Tbsp.	fish sauce	30 mL
1 1/2 tsp.	sugar	7.5 mL
5 Tbsp.	lime juice	75 mL
1/4 tsp.	salt	1.2 mL
1/2 tsp.	black pepper	2.5 mL

Preheat the oven to 350°F (175°C). Place the potatoes in a pot and cover with water. Bring to a boil and cook until the potatoes are tender, about 20 minutes. Drain and cool. Lightly oil the beets and carrots. Place in separate areas on a baking sheet and roast for about 45 minutes or until they are tender. Remove from the oven and let stand until cool enough to handle.

Peel the potatoes and cut into 1-inch (2.5-cm) cubes. Place in a large bowl. Peel the carrots and slice into thin rounds. Add them to the potatoes. Peel the beets, cut into 1/2-inch (1.2-cm) cubes and reserve. Peel and coarsely chop the hard-cooked eggs. Add to the potatoes and carrots. Add the celery hearts, green onion, cilantro and mint.

Heat the vegetable oil in a very small pan over medium heat. Add the garlic and cook until it just starts to turn golden. Remove from the heat.

In a small bowl, combine the fish sauce, sugar, lime juice, salt and pepper. Stir well to dissolve the salt and sugar. Add the garlic and vegetable oil. Pour over the salad and mix well. Add the beets and mix again. Let stand for an hour or so before serving.

Whole Artichokes with Honey Caper Mayonnaise

This combination came to me while preparing Steven's Birthday Dinner one year. Artichokes from California are at their peak in February and are a Birthday must. I served them as a first course with three different types of mayonnaise—curry, sesame, and honey caper, which was everybody's favorite, hands down. If using raw eggs makes you uncomfortable, stir 2 tsp. (10 mL) lemon juice, the honey and the capers into 1 1/4 cups (300 mL) prepared mayonnaise.

Serves 4

1	lemon, cut in half	1
4	large, fresh artichokes	4
1 recipe	Honey Caper Mayonnaise	1 recipe

Have a large bowl of cold water at hand. Squeeze half the lemon into the water.

Trim the artichokes by snapping off the bottom layer of leaves. Cut off the top 1 inch (2.5 cm) of the artichoke with a serrated knife. Trim the points of the bottom leaves with scissors. Rub all the cut surfaces with the other half of the lemon.

Trim the stem and peel it with a vegetable peeler or a small knife. Rub with lemon and drop into the bowl of water. Continue with the remaining artichokes.

Transfer the artichokes to a large pot and cover with cold water. Bring to a boil and cook until the bases are tender when pierced with a knife, 30-40 minutes. Drain and turn the artichokes upside down to cool. Refrigerate until cold, about 1 hour. The artichokes may be prepared a day in advance. Cover and refrigerate.

To serve, place each artichoke on a plate and serve with a ramekin of the mayonnaise. Pull off a leaf at a time and dip into the mayonnaise. Pull the leaf through your teeth to extract the tender flesh on the bottom. When you reach the choke, remove the spiky, purple-tinged leaves to expose the fuzzy choke. Scrape out the choke with the tip of a knife or a small spoon. Cut the heart into quarters and enjoy.

Honey Caper Mayonnaise

To make it by hand, whisk the egg yolks, salt and mustard together in a medium-sized bowl. Whisking constantly, add the oil, drop by drop, until it is all incorporated and the mixture is emulsified. Whisk in the lemon juice, honey and capers.

Makes 1 1/3 cups (320 mL)

3	large egg yolks	3
1/2 tsp.	salt	2.5 mL
1 tsp.	Dijon mustard	5 mL
1/2 cup	olive oil	120 mL
1/2 cup	vegetable oil	120 mL
4 tsp.	lemon juice	20 mL
1 Tbsp.	fragrant honey	15 mL
2 tsp.	small capers	10 mL

Place the egg yolks in a food processor or blender. Add the salt and mustard. With the motor running, slowly dribble the olive and vegetable oils into the egg yolks. If the mixture seems too thick at any point, add a bit of water. When all the oil has been incorporated and the mixture is emulsified, add the lemon juice. Transfer to a bowl and stir in the honey and capers. Cover and refrigerate for up to 3 days.

Wok-Seared Bean Sprouts

Technique is the most important ingredient here. The pan has to be smokingly hot before adding the oil and bean sprouts, to give them a desirable smoky edge. Perfect with Chicken Steamed with Ginger and Sherry, page 25.

Serves 2-3

1 Tbsp.	vegetable oil	15 mL
1 lb.	bean sprouts	454 g
1/2 tsp.	salt	2.5 mL
	pinch of sugar	
1 Tbsp.	Chinese cooking wine or dry sherry	15 mL
4 tsp.	light soy sauce	20 mL

Heat a heavy wok or cast-iron frying pan over high heat until smoking. Add the oil, then the bean sprouts. Let them sit for a minute, until a thin dark line forms on the sprouts that are in contact with the pan. Flip the sprouts over and sear them for another minute. Sprinkle with the salt and sugar and stir-fry for a minute. Splash on the wine, stir and fry, and when it has almost evaporated, add the soy sauce. Stir and fry until the sprouts are tender-crisp. Transfer to a heated plate and serve immediately.

Braised Sugar Snap Peas with Mint

Like traditional braised peas with mint, this uses succulent and easily prepared sugar snap peas.

Serves 4

10	large leaves of butter lettuce	10
1 lb.	sugar snap peas, stringed	454 g
2 Tbsp.	unsalted butter	30 mL
	pinch of sugar	
	salt to taste	
20	sprigs fresh mint	20
4	green onions	4

Wash the lettuce and arrange half the leaves in a medium-sized pot with a tight-fitting lid. Add the peas, butter, sugar and a sprinkling of salt. Tie the mint and green onions together and bury in the peas. Cover with the remaining lettuce.

Cook over medium heat until it's steaming, then turn the heat to low and cover with a lid. Cook, shaking the pan occasionally, until the peas are just tender, about 5 minutes. Remove and discard the bundle of mint and onions. Serve with the lettuce leaves.

Stir-Fried Swiss Chard with Garlic, Anchovies and Raisins

I love this with roasted chicken and mashed potatoes or crispy pan-roasted salmon.

Serves 4

1 Tbsp.	golden raisins	15 mL
2 tsp.	balsamic vinegar	10 mL
2 tsp.	water	10 mL
1 Tbsp.	olive oil	15 mL
3	medium cloves garlic, minced	3
3	anchovies, finely chopped	3
1	dried hot red pepper, finely chopped	1
2	medium bunches Swiss chard, washed and dried, leaves coarsely chopped and stems thinly sliced	2
	salt and pepper to taste	

In a small frying pan, combine the raisins, balsamic vinegar and water. Bring to a boil and remove from the heat. Cover and let stand while preparing the rest of the ingredients.

Heat a wok or heavy frying pan over high heat. Add the oil and garlic and stir-fry for 10 seconds. Add the anchovies and hot pepper and stir well. Add the Swiss chard and stir-fry over high heat until it wilts. Turn the heat to medium and continue stir-frying until the chard is tender. Add the raisins and balsamic vinegar and season with salt and pepper.

Penne with Fresh Artichokes, Asparagus, Spinach and Prosciutto

The perfect spring pasta. If you wish, add some fresh peas with the artichokes and asparagus.

Trimming Artichokes

To trim an artichoke down to the heart, prepare a large bowl of water to which you have added the juice of one lemon. First snap off all the leaves by bending them down toward the base. As you get closer to the center, the leaves become more tender and you will be able to snap off a few at a time. The middle of the artichoke has beautiful, translucent pale green and purple leaves. Grasp them firmly and pull them out too. Under this you will find the furry choke. With a small spoon, scrape out the choke. The next step is to trim the outside and stem of the artichoke with a small sharp knife. Trim the end of the stem and carefully start peeling off the dark green skin. The newly trimmed artichoke heart will be a pale green. Drop it into the lemon water to prevent it from discoloring.

Serves 4

2	large, fresh artichokes, trimmed down to their hearts	2
3/4 lb.	fat asparagus, woody ends snapped off	340 g
1/2 lb.	fresh spinach, stemmed, washed and drained	227 g
4 Tbsp.	olive oil	60 mL
4	cloves garlic, thinly sliced	4
4	thin slices prosciutto	4
1/2 cup	chicken stock	120 mL
1/2 cup	white wine	120 mL
1/8 tsp.	salt	.5 mL
1 lb.	penne	454 g
1/2 cup	freshly grated Parmesan cheese or grana padano	120 mL
2 Tbsp.	fresh chives, finely chopped freshly ground black pepper to taste	30 mL

Cut each artichoke heart into eight wedges. Cut the asparagus into 1 1/2-inch (3.8-cm) diagonal pieces. Cut the spinach into very thin strips and set aside.

Heat the olive oil in a large frying pan over medium heat. Add the garlic and prosciutto and sauté just until the garlic begins to turn golden. Add the artichoke pieces and asparagus and cook for a moment. Add the chicken stock, wine and salt. Cook over high heat until the liquid is reduced by half and the artichokes are tender. Remove from the heat.

While you are preparing the sauce, bring a large pot of water to a boil. Salt liberally. It should taste like seawater. Add the penne and cook, stirring occasionally, until the pasta is cooked but still firm to the bite. Drain the pasta and quickly reheat the sauce. Add the pasta to the sauce along with the spinach. Toss and stir until the spinach wilts. Add the grated cheese, chives and pepper. Stir a few more times to incorporate the ingredients and serve immediately in heated bowls.

Orzo with Lemon and Herbs

Orzo, like any pasta, is adaptable to many seasonings. It can be served where you would have rice or pasta with a main course.

Serves 4

1 1/4 cups	orzo	300 mL
1/2 cup	chicken stock	120 mL
1 Tbsp.	unsalted butter	15 mL
1 Tbsp.	olive oil	15 mL
1 Tbsp.	fresh parsley, finely chopped	15 mL
1 Tbsp.	fresh mint, finely chopped	15 mL
2 tsp.	fresh thyme leaves, finely chopped	10 mL
2 tsp.	lemon zest	10 mL
1 Tbsp.	freshly squeezed lemon juice	15 mL
	salt and pepper to taste	

Bring a large pot of water to a boil. Add the orzo and salt the water liberally. It should taste like seawater. Cook until the orzo is tender, 8-10 minutes. Drain and return to the pot.

While the orzo is cooking, combine the chicken stock, butter and olive oil in a small pot. Bring to a boil and remove from the heat. Add to the cooked orzo along with the fresh herbs, lemon zest and juice, salt and pepper. Mix well and serve.

Asparagus Risotto

Instead of stock, I like to use the asparagus cooking water for extra flavor. This technique can be adopted for any vegetable risotto.

Serves 4

1 lb.	asparagus	454 g
6 cups	water	1.5 L
2 Tbsp.	olive oil	30 mL
1/2 cup	onion, finely chopped	120 mL
1 1/2 cups	arborio rice	360 mL
	salt and pepper to taste	
1 Tbsp.	unsalted butter	15 mL
1/2 cup	freshly grated Parmesan cheese	120 mL
	zest of 1/2 lemon	

Snap or cut the fibrous ends from the asparagus and discard. Cut the spears into 1-inch (2.5-cm) lengths on the bias. Bring the water to a boil, add the asparagus and cook until it is bright green and still crisp, 2 minutes. Remove with a slotted spoon to a colander. Cool under cold water and set aside. Turn the asparagus water down to a simmer.

In a large, heavy-bottomed pot, heat the olive oil over medium heat. Add the onion and cook, stirring frequently, until the onion is soft but not browned. Add the rice and stir to coat it with the oil. Add 1/2 cup (120 mL) of the asparagus water and cook, stirring constantly, until the water is absorbed and the rice is creamy. Continue stirring, adding the asparagus water by half-cups until the rice is very tender but still firm to the bite. Season with salt and pepper. Add the asparagus and stir in the butter, cheese and lemon zest. Serve immediately in heated bowls.

Asparagus Frittata

Frittatas make a nice easy dinner with a salad and good bread. They are adaptable too—you can add a spoonful of pesto or a few chopped sun-dried tomatoes to the egg mixture.

Serves 4

2 Tbsp.	olive oil	30 mL
1/2 cup	onion, thinly sliced	120 mL
1	clove garlic, minced	1
1 tsp.	fresh thyme, chopped	5 mL
1	large tomato, seeded and diced	1
1/4 lb.	new red potatoes, cooked, cooled and cut into 1/2-inch (1.2-cm) dice	113 g
12	cooked asparagus stalks, cut into 2-inch (5-cm) pieces	12
8	large eggs	8
1/2 tsp.	salt	2.5 mL
1/2 tsp.	pepper	2.5 mL
1/2 cup	freshly grated Parmesan cheese	120 mL
1	green onion, thinly sliced	1

Heat 1 Tbsp. (15 mL) of the olive oil over medium heat in a large, preferably nonstick, ovenproof frying pan. Add the onion, garlic and thyme. Sauté until the onion is soft. Add half the tomato and the potatoes and cook until the potatoes are heated through, 4-5 minutes. Add the asparagus and cook for a minute longer. Remove the vegetables and wipe out the pan.

Turn on the broiler. While it is heating, beat the eggs, salt, pepper and cheese together. Heat the remaining oil over medium heat. Pour in the eggs and scatter the vegetables on top of the eggs. Turn the heat to low and cook until the frittata is golden brown on the bottom, 5-8 minutes. Place the frittata under the broiler and cook until firm. Slide onto a plate and garnish with the remaining chopped tomato and green onion.

Chickpea, Rice and Spinach Soup with Lemon and Mint

This easy and delicious soup may be garnished with yogurt if you like.

Serves 4

6 cups	chicken stock	1.5 L
1	15-oz. (420-mL) can chickpeas, drained and rinsed	1
1 cup	cooked rice	240 mL
4	cloves garlic, minced	4
1/2 tsp.	turmeric	2.5 mL
1/2 tsp.	whole cumin seeds	2.5 mL
1/2 lb.	fresh spinach, stems removed and washed	227 g
2	large eggs	2
1/2 cup	freshly squeezed lemon juice	120 mL
	salt and pepper to taste	
2 Tbsp.	fresh mint, finely chopped	30 mL

Combine the chicken stock, chickpeas, rice, garlic, turmeric and cumin in a large pot. Bring to a boil and simmer for 15-20 minutes. Finely chop the spinach and add it to the soup. Beat the eggs and lemon juice together. Whisk 1 cup (240 mL) of the hot soup into the egg mixture. Over low heat, slowly whisk the egg mixture into the soup. Do not let it boil. Stir until the soup is piping hot. Season with salt and pepper. Ladle into warm bowls and garnish with mint.

Rhubarb Meringue Custard Pie

For me, rhubarb is the true sign of spring, both physically and symbolically. In the Middle East, it is added to lentil soups for an edge of sourness. Here we tend to combat the sourness with sugar, as in this pie.

Makes 1 9-inch (23-cm) pie

1 recipe	Flaky Pastry (page 206)	1 recipe
3/4 cup	sugar	180 mL
4 Tbsp.	unsalted butter, at room temperature	60 mL
2	large eggs	2
1/4 cup	milk	60 mL
1 tsp.	pure vanilla extract	5 mL
1 1/2 lbs.	rhubarb, trimmed and cut into 1-inch (2.5-cm) pieces	680 g
2 Tbsp.	flour	30 mL
3	large egg whites	3
1/4 tsp.	cream of tartar	1.2 mL
1/2 cup	sugar	120 mL

Make the pastry, following the instructions on how to prebake a pie crust, and using a 9-inch (23-cm) pie pan. Bake for 10 minutes only and cool completely. Adjust the oven temperature to 375°F (190°C).

Beat the sugar and butter together until fluffy. Beat in the eggs one at a time, then the milk and vanilla. Toss the rhubarb with the flour and stir into the sugar mixture. Pour into the cooled pie crust and bake until just set in the middle, about 1 1/4 hours. Place on a rack and cool to room temperature.

For the meringue, beat the egg whites on medium speed until they become frothy. Add the cream of tartar and beat on high speed until they form soft peaks. Gradually add the sugar and beat until stiff and shiny. Cover the cooled pie with the meringue, making sure that it touches the pie crust all the way around. This anchors the meringue and prevents it from slipping after it is baked. Bake until the top is lightly browned, 10-15 minutes. Cool completely before serving.

Rhubarb Cake

Serve this warm, with vanilla ice cream.

Makes 1 8-inch (20-cm) square cake

2 cups	flour	475 mL
1 cup	sugar	240 mL
4 tsp.	baking powder	20 mL
1/2 tsp.	salt	2.5 mL
1	large egg	1
1 cup	yogurt	240 mL
1/4 cup	unsalted butter, melted	60 mL
2 tsp.	pure vanilla extract	10 mL
1/2 lb.	rhubarb, trimmed and cut into 1-inch (2.5-cm) pieces	227 g
1/4 cup	brown sugar	60 mL
1 Tbsp.	flour	15 mL
1/2 tsp.	cinnamon	2.5 mL
1 Tbsp.	unsalted butter, at room temperature	15 mL

Preheat the oven to 350°F (175°C). Butter and flour an 8-inch (20-cm) square pan.

Sift the flour, sugar, baking powder and salt together. Beat the egg, yogurt, melted butter and vanilla together. Whisk into the flour mixture until just blended. Fold in the rhubarb. Spread into the prepared pan. Combine the brown sugar, flour and cinnamon. Work in the butter with your fingertips till crumbly. Sprinkle over the cake. Bake for 45-50 minutes, until a cake tester comes out clean. Cool on a wire rack and serve warm.

Panna Cotta Latte-da

Yes, I too jumped on the panna cotta bandwagon. Although it never caught on like the pandemic tiramisu or crème brûlée, it still is a lovely, simple dessert. Panna is "cream" in Italian and cotta means "cooked." This is a coffee-flavored version. Instead of using ramekins, you can vary the shape by using teacups, small bowls or even martini glasses.

Serves 6

1 3/4 cups	whipping cream	425 mL
1/3 cup	milk	80 mL
1/4 cup	sugar	60 mL
2 1/2 tsp.	gelatin	12.5 mL
2 Tbsp.	water	30 mL
1/2 cup	brewed espresso	120 mL
1 tsp.	pure vanilla extract	5 mL
2 Tbsp.	coffee-flavored liqueur or Irish cream liqueur	30 mL
2 tsp.	instant coffee granules	10 mL

Rinse six 1/2-cup (120-mL) ramekins in cold water but do not dry them.

In a heavy-bottomed pot, heat the cream, milk and sugar over medium heat. Simmer for 5 minutes, stirring occasionally. Meanwhile, sprinkle the gelatin over the water. When it is soft, stir it into the cream mixture until dissolved. Remove from the heat and stir in the espresso, vanilla, liqueur and instant coffee. Pour into the ramekins and cool. Refrigerate for at least 4 hours or up to 3 days, covered.

To unmold, dip each ramekin in a bowl of hot water for 10 seconds. Run a thin knife around the panna cotta and invert onto plates. Serve with a dusting of cocoa, if desired.

Lemon Crumb Cake with Lemon Curd

You can serve this with whipping cream if you don't have time to make lemon curd.

Makes 1 8-inch (20-cm) square cake

2 cups	flour	475 mL
1 cup	sugar	240 mL
1/2 cup	well-packed light brown sugar	120 mL
2 Tbsp.	lemon zest, finely chopped	30 mL
1/4 tsp.	ground nutmeg	1.2 mL
1/2 cup	vegetable oil	120 mL
4 Tbsp.	freshly squeezed lemon juice	60 mL
1 cup	sour cream	240 mL
1	large egg	1
1 tsp.	pure vanilla extract	5 mL
1 tsp.	baking soda	5 mL
1 tsp.	baking powder	5 mL

Preheat the oven to 325°F (165°C). Lightly butter and flour an 8-inch (20-cm) glass baking dish. Whisk together the flour, sugars, lemon zest and nutmeg. Whisk in the oil and lemon juice until it forms a lumpy mixture. Reserve 1 cup (240 mL). Combine the sour cream, egg, vanilla, baking soda and baking powder. Whisk into the flour mixture or beat with an electric mixer until smooth. Spread into the pan and sprinkle the reserved mixture over the top. Bake for 35-40 minutes until a cake tester comes out clean. Serve with a dollop of Lemon Curd.

Lemon Curd

This is great to have on hand to spread on toast. You can thin it out with a bit of cream or water for a quick lemon sauce.

Makes about 2 cups

4	large eggs	4
1 cup	sugar	240 mL
2/3 cup	lemon juice (about 4 lemons)	160 mL
	zest of 2 lemons, finely chopped	2
1/2 cup	unsalted butter, cut into small pieces	120 mL

Whip the eggs and sugar together until doubled in volume and light in color. Stir in the lemon juice and zest. Transfer to the top of a double boiler and cook over simmering water until very thick, about 20-30 minutes, stirring occasionally with a whisk. Remove from the heat and add the butter, stirring until melted. Cool and refrigerate. Will keep for a month in the refrigerator.

Summer

Feast for Your First Day of Summer

Lemon and Lavender Roasted Chicken

Spoon Bread

J.R.'s Iceberg Wedges with Blue Cheese Dressing

Green Beans with Salsa

Coconut Cream Pie

*T*his feast doesn't have to happen on the real first day, of course. It can happen when you are ready to celebrate it. For me, it's around the May long weekend. We have had it at home and at picnics, and sometimes we repeat it in August, or for a special summer occasion.

It has evolved over the years, like any good feast. Fried chicken was once the order of the day—fried to crunchy heaven in a cast-iron pan of lard, with cream gravy made from the crispy bits in the bottom of the pan. In the interest of good digestion, this gave way to lemon-roasted chicken, and we now reminisce about how good the fried chicken was.

The feast is a leisurely one to prepare. The chicken is marinated the day before and the beans are trimmed. The blue cheese dressing and pie filling can be made a few days in advance. The pie crust can be rolled and frozen until ready to bake. The spoon bread, salsa for the beans, pie crust and chicken are cooked the day of the feast and the pie is assembled. If you want a feast with no last-minute cooking, or a portable feast, serve the chicken at room temperature and make Potato and Grilled Corn Salad with Buttermilk Cilantro Dressing, page 88.

Lemon and Lavender Roasted Chicken

*L*avender is an under-utilized herb, generally relegated to the undie drawer. This is most unfortunate, since fresh lavender has a honey-like flavor and intriguing aroma. It pairs with chicken but is also excellent with fish. It is one of the components of the French herb mixture Herbes de Provence.

Serves 6-8

3/4 cup	freshly squeezed lemon juice	180 mL
4 Tbsp.	olive oil	60 mL
8	cloves garlic, minced	8
1 Tbsp.	salt	15 mL
1 Tbsp.	coarsely ground black pepper	15 mL
2 Tbsp.	fresh lavender leaves, coarsely chopped	30 mL
1 Tbsp.	fresh thyme leaves	15 mL
4	2 1/2-3 lbs. (1.1-1.4 kg) chickens, split down the back and flattened	4

Combine the lemon juice, olive oil, garlic, salt, pepper, lavender, and thyme. Spread over the top and bottom of the chickens, making sure they are evenly coated, and place them in a large bowl. Cover and refrigerate overnight.

Preheat the oven to 425°F (220°C). Transfer the chickens and the marinade to two pans that will fit the chickens comfortably, and bake, basting occasionally with the marinade, until cooked through and golden brown, 50-60 minutes. Cut immediately into halves or quarters if you are serving them hot, or wait until they cool before cutting if you are serving them cold.

Spoon Bread

Spoon bread, an American tradition in southern states, is a cross between a soufflé and a pudding. It is made with white cornmeal, which is almost impossible to find here, so yellow cornmeal will suffice. It can be made with or without the corn and deserves to be a tradition everywhere.

Serves 6-8

3	fresh ears of corn	3
3 cups	milk	720 mL
2 tsp.	salt	10 mL
1 Tbsp.	sugar	15 mL
1 cup	cornmeal	240 mL
6 Tbsp.	unsalted butter	90 mL
3	eggs, separated	3
	a few shakes Tabasco sauce	

Preheat the oven to 350°F (175°C). Butter a 9- by 13-inch (23- by 33-cm) baking dish.

Into a bowl, slice the corn from the cob in thin slices, rather than cutting the kernels off right at the cob. What you want is small bits of corn, not whole kernels. Scrape the cobs to extract all the liquid.

Transfer the corn and its liquid to a large heavy saucepan. Add 2 cups (475 ml) of the milk, the salt and sugar and bring to a boil. Slowly whisk in the cornmeal. Reduce the heat to low and cook, stirring frequently, until thick, about 10 minutes. Stir in the butter, then the remaining milk. Remove from the heat and quickly beat in the egg yolks and Tabasco sauce.

Beat the egg whites until stiff but not dry and fold into the cornmeal mixture. Scrape into the buttered baking dish and bake for 25-30 minutes, until barely set in the middle. Remove from the oven and serve hot.

J.R.'s Iceberg Wedges with Blue Cheese Dressing

*J*ohn Reese, the general manager of the Fish House, and I were smitten by this salad and contemplated putting it on the menu. After much deliberation, we realized that we could never get away with it—it was too old and too new at the same time. But in our minds, it will always be high fashion.

Serves 8

4 oz.	blue cheese, crumbled	113 g
1 cup	sour cream	240 mL
1/4 cup	mayonnaise	60 mL
2 tsp.	minced garlic	10 mL
1 Tbsp.	red wine vinegar	15 mL
	salt and pepper to taste	
1	head iceberg lettuce, cut into 8 wedges	

Mix all the ingredients except the lettuce in a bowl. Cover and refrigerate overnight or for up to one week. Taste and adjust the seasoning. Place the iceberg wedges on chilled individual plates. Spoon the dressing over the lettuce before serving, or pass the dressing separately.

Green Beans with Salsa

A fresh and novel approach to green beans. It can be served hot or cold.

Serves 6-8

2 lbs.	green beans, trimmed	900 g
1 lb.	ripe plum tomatoes, peeled and finely chopped	454 g
1/2 cup	white onion, finely diced	120 mL
1	clove garlic, minced	1
1 Tbsp.	fresh cilantro, finely chopped	15 mL
1	jalapeño or serrano chili, finely chopped	1
2 Tbsp.	fresh lime juice	30 mL
	salt to taste	
2 Tbsp.	olive oil	30 mL

Bring a large pot of water to a boil and add the green beans. Cook until they are bright green and still very crisp, 3-4 minutes. Drain and cool under cold water. Drain well and pat dry.

Combine the tomatoes, onion, garlic, cilantro, chili and lime juice and season well with salt. The recipe may be prepared up to 1 day in advance to this point. Cover and refrigerate. Before proceeding, drain the salsa through a sieve.

In a large heavy frying pan, heat the oil over high heat until it is very hot but not smoking. Add the salsa and stir and fry until it thickens, 3-4 minutes. Add the green beans and cook until the beans are heated through but still crisp, 3-4 minutes. Transfer to a platter and serve hot or at room temperature.

Coconut Cream Pie

This pie has been a staple for years and made it onto the Fish House menu when it first re-opened in 1995. When it came time to change to the fall menu, I took it off, thinking it was too summery. The servers circulated a petition, demanding the pie be put back on the menu because it was easy to sell and well loved by all who ate it. It has remained on the menu ever since, and continues to please.

Serves 6-8

1	fully baked 9-inch (23-cm) pie shell (see Flaky Pastry, page 206)	1
2 cups	sweetened, long-shred coconut	475 mL
1/2 cup	sugar	120 mL
2	large eggs	2
2 Tbsp.	flour	30 mL
	pinch of salt	
2 cups	milk	475 mL
2 Tbsp.	unsalted butter	30 mL
1 tsp.	pure vanilla extract	5 mL
1 cup	whipping cream	240 mL

Have a prebaked pie shell ready. Preheat the oven to 350°F (175°C). Spread 1/2 cup (120 mL) of the coconut onto a baking sheet and toast, watching carefully, until it is golden brown, about 3-5 minutes. Remove and cool. Place the remaining coconut in the freezer.

Beat the sugar, eggs, flour and salt together until smooth. Heat the milk in a large, heavy pot until just below the boiling point. Whisk the milk slowly into the egg mixture, then return it to the pot. Stir constantly over high heat with a rubber spatula until the mixture comes to a boil. Immediately remove from the heat and stir in the chilled coconut (the chilled coconut stops the cooking and prevents curdling). Scrape into a bowl and stir in the butter and vanilla. Cool completely. Cover and refrigerate until cold, or up to 3 days.

A few hours before you serve the pie, but not too early or the crust will get soggy, transfer the cold coconut mixture to the baked pie shell and smooth out the top. Whip the cream until soft peaks form and swirl it over the top of the pie. Sprinkle with the toasted coconut and refrigerate until ready to serve.

Feast for the Longest Day

Pine Nut and Parsley Salad

Cracked and Cooked Olive Salad

Fanatic's Hummous

Whole Roasted Eggplant with
Tomatoes and Capers

Grilled Zucchini with Mint, Yogurt
and Feta Cheese

Vegetable Platter

Pita Bread

Almond Granita

One of the particularly wonderful things about summer is the profusion of fresh vegetables, and one of the best ways to serve them is in the Middle Eastern tradition of *mezze*—small dishes of food to nibble on as you please. The cooking is leisurely, and everything is served at room temperature on small plates. Eating is communal and everyone uses pita bread in place of knives or forks. I like a profusion of dishes that guests can munch at as they wish. In addition to the pita bread, I like to have a platter of fresh vegetables for dipping and scooping. Cucumbers, tomatoes, radishes, inner hearts of

romaine lettuce, pickled hot peppers and onion is traditional and the most tasty accompaniment. If you have my first book, *Pacific Passions,* you could add Garden Antipasto or Smoked Eggplant Purée to the feast. Serve all the dishes on small plates or platters, one for each end of the table.

The key to pleasant feasting is organization. If several recipes use the same ingredient, peel or chop it in advance. Read over the recipes you are using and make a game plan as to how far in advance a recipe or elements of it can be prepared and do it over a few days. Vinaigrettes or dressings. can be made, garlic and onion can be peeled. Don't chop tomatoes or cucumbers in advance: they lose their fresh taste and become soggy. Prepare, cover and refrigerate your ingredients until ready to use. This is the leisurely way. On the feast day, you will be left with a small amount of cooking and can concentrate on setting the table or sitting in the sun.

Pine Nut and Parsley Salad

I love this interpretation of tabouli. If you are concerned about the price of pine nuts, remember that this feast is based on vegetables, and therefore is very inexpensive to prepare. If you want a regular tabouli, rinse 1/2 cup (120 mL) fine bulgar in a sieve, drain well and add to the salad just before tossing with the dressing.

Serves 8

2 Tbsp.	vegetable oil	30 mL
1 cup	pine nuts	240 mL
1 cup	fresh mint leaves, coarsely chopped	240 mL
2 cups	fresh parsley, finely chopped	475 mL
1/3 cup	tomatoes, seeded and finely chopped	80 mL
1/3 cup	English cucumber, seeded and finely diced	80 mL
1/4 cup	green onion, thinly sliced	60 mL
2 Tbsp.	freshly squeezed lemon juice	30 mL
1/2 tsp.	salt	2.5 mL
1/2 tsp.	garlic, finely chopped	2.5 mL
5 Tbsp.	olive oil	75 mL
1/4 tsp.	ground cinnamon	1.2 mL
1/2 tsp.	ground allspice	2.5 mL

In a small frying pan, heat the vegetable oil over low heat. Add the pine nuts and sauté, stirring constantly until pale gold. Remove from the heat and drain off the oil through a sieve. Cool.

Combine the mint, parsley, tomatoes, cucumber and green onion. For the dressing, combine the lemon juice, salt and garlic in a small bowl. Stir well. Slowly beat in the olive oil. Stir in the cinnamon and allspice. The vegetables may be prepared 4-6 hours in advance. Cover and refrigerate. Just before serving, toss with the pine nuts and dressing.

Cracked and Cooked Olive Salad

This is a good condiment to have around for spreading on bread or adding to pastas.

Makes 3 1/2 cups (765 mL)

1 lb.	whole, good-quality green olives	454 g
1/3 cup	olive oil	80 mL
2 Tbsp.	minced garlic	30 mL
2 cups	well-drained, canned plum tomatoes, finely chopped	475 mL
1 Tbsp.	tomato paste	15 mL
1/2 cup	water	120 mL
4	thin slices lemon, seeds removed	4
1 tsp.	paprika	5 mL
1/2 tsp.	cayenne pepper	2.5 mL
1 tsp.	ground coriander seeds	5 mL
1/2 tsp.	ground cumin seeds	2.5 mL

Using the flat of a large heavy knife, whack each olive to split it in half. Remove the pits and discard. Combine the olives, olive oil, garlic, tomatoes, tomato paste and water in a heavy pot. Bring to a boil, turn down to a simmer and simmer for 5 minutes, stirring frequently. Add the lemon slices, paprika, cayenne, coriander and cumin. Simmer, stirring frequently, until the mixture clings to the olives, about 10 minutes. Cool. Cover and refrigerate until ready to serve.

Whole Roasted Eggplant with Tomatoes and Capers

This is a beautiful presentation for small eggplants, roasted whole and sprinkled with mint leaves. When peeling the eggplants, leave a few strips of peel here and there. This adds to the appearance of the dish.

Serves 8

8	small Japanese eggplants, about 3 lbs. (1.4 kg), peeled, but with stem end left on	8
6 Tbsp.	olive oil	90 mL
4 Tbsp.	freshly squeezed lemon juice	60 mL
1/2 tsp.	salt	2.5 mL
1 Tbsp.	drained capers	15 mL
2	cloves garlic, minced	2
	pinch of cinnamon	
2	large ripe tomatoes, peeled, seeded and coarsely chopped	2
1/2 cup	fresh parsley, coarsely chopped	120 mL
1/2 cup	fresh mint, coarsely chopped	120 mL

Preheat the oven to 400°F (200°C). Combine the eggplants and olive oil in a large bowl and toss well to coat. Transfer the eggplants to a rimmed baking sheet, well apart, and bake for 30-40 minutes, turning occasionally, until the eggplant is soft and browned.

Transfer to a 9- by 13-inch (23- by 33-cm) glass baking dish, leaving any olive oil behind on the baking sheet. Mix the lemon juice, salt, capers, garlic and cinnamon together in a small bowl. Pour over the eggplant, turning to coat it with the lemon juice mixture. Cool to room temperature. Cover and refrigerate until ready to serve, up to 2 days.

Transfer the eggplant to a serving platter. Combine the tomatoes, parsley and mint. Sprinkle over the eggplant. Serve at room temperature.

Grilled Zucchini with Yogurt, Mint and Feta Cheese

Although you can drain the yogurt a couple of days in advance, the dish is best assembled just before serving.

Serves 8

1 1/2 cups	plain natural yogurt	360 mL
8	small zucchini, about 2 lbs. (900 g)	8
2 Tbsp.	olive oil	30 mL
	salt to taste	
2 Tbsp.	water	30 mL
1	clove garlic, minced	1
1/4 tsp.	salt	1.2 mL
1/2 cup	crumbled feta cheese	120 mL
1/2 cup	fresh mint leaves, coarsely chopped	120 mL

Line a sieve with a double layer of paper towels. Add the yogurt and let it drain for 1 1/2 hours. Transfer to a bowl, cover and refrigerate until ready to use. Discard the liquid.

Preheat the barbecue or broiler to high. Trim the zucchini, cut it in half lengthwise and toss with the olive oil and salt. Grill or broil the zucchini, turning once, until tender and browned. Transfer to a colander, cut side down, to drain and cool.

Combine the yogurt with the water, garlic and 1/4 tsp. (1.2 ml) salt. Transfer the cooled zucchini to a serving platter. Drizzle the yogurt mixture over the zucchini; sprinkle with the feta cheese and mint.

Fanatic's Hummous

Why fanatic? I peel the chickpeas. It isn't difficult and you don't need a chickpea peeler. Just pop off the skins between your thumb and first finger. The reward: a hummous that is smooth like silk!

Serves 8

1	28-oz. (796-mL) can chickpeas, drained and rinsed	1
1/4 cup	water	60 mL
1/2 cup	tahini	120 mL
1/4 -1/2 cup	freshly squeezed lemon juice	60-120 mL
2	cloves garlic, minced	2
1/2 tsp.	salt	2.5 mL

Peel the chickpeas as described at left. Place in a food processor or blender with the water and blend until completely smooth. Add the tahini and the smaller amount of lemon juice, garlic and salt. Blend until well combined. Add more lemon juice and salt to your taste. Refrigerate, covered, until serving time.

Almond Granita

A simple to make, very refreshing dessert.

Serves 8

2 cups	whole almonds, skin on, roasted and cooled	475 mL
4 cups	water	950 mL
1 1/2 cups	sugar	360 mL
3/4 cup	light corn syrup	180 mL
2 tsp.	grated lemon zest	10 mL
4 Tbsp.	almond-flavored liqueur	60 mL

Pulse the almonds to a powder in a food processor. Transfer to a pot and combine with the water, sugar, corn syrup and lemon zest. Bring to a boil over medium heat, stirring occasionally. Cool completely and add the liqueur. Transfer to a 9- by 13-inch (23- by 33-cm) glass baking dish and place in the freezer. Freeze for 3 hours, stirring with a whisk every 30 minutes, until the granita has completely frozen into small granules. Serve the same day or cover and keep frozen for up to 2 days. Stir with a fork to break up the granita before serving.

The Ultimate in Surf and Turf

Crusty Rib-eye Steaks

White Clam Linguine

I have always thought of surf and turf as an odd and frivolous combination of flavors and textures. The seafood never seems to stand up well to the beef. Other combinations that equally baffle me are ribs and spaghetti, steak and lasagne, chicken and tortellini, and so on. But it usually happens that whenever I make fun of something, I end up becoming so intrigued by it that I have to start cooking it—so with this combination, it was the double whammy of surf and turf *and* steak and spaghetti. In this case, the heady clam pasta can really hold its own against the steak.

Crusty Rib-eye Steaks

I like rib-eye steaks to be at least 12 ounces (340 g) each. You can split it two or three ways if you want, but it has to be thick, thick, thick. I use the grilling sauce that I use for My Birthday Ribs, with several spoonfuls of mayonnaise added, right out of the jar (now you can laugh at my food preferences). I grill the steaks on high so they get nice and crusty. This is where the mayonnaise helps. You can prepare the steaks in your usual way, with the cut you prefer, or use my method.

Serves 4

3 Tbsp.	ketchup	45 mL
3 Tbsp.	oyster sauce	45 mL
3 Tbsp.	saté sauce (see page 13)	45 mL
1/2 tsp.	Worcestershire sauce	2.5 mL
4 Tbsp.	prepared mayonnaise	60 mL
4	12 oz. (340 g) rib-eye steaks	4

Stir all of the ingredients except the steaks together and smear all over the steaks. Preheat the barbecue to high. Cook the steaks, turning over once, about 3-4 minutes on each side for medium rare. See How Do I Know When It's Done?, page 119. Serve immediately on piping hot plates, beside the White Clam Linguine. Surf and Turf Heaven!

White Clam Linguine

*D*on't save this for surf and turf; it is divine any time!

How Can I Stop Pasta From Sticking Together?

I've never understood adding oil to pasta water. Think about it—the oil floats on top of the water. How does it get near the pasta? The main reason pasta sticks is because the pot is too small. Pasta needs a lot of water to cook properly, 5-6 quarts (5-6 L) per pound (454 g) of pasta. The water has to boil rapidly, so if you have a burner that is stronger than the rest, use it. A tall, narrow pot is better than a short, wide pot because the heat will be distributed up through the water, which keeps it boiling rapidly. After adding the pasta to the boiling water, stir it up from the bottom as soon as it starts to bend and stir occasionally while it is cooking. Stay away from those pots that have strainer baskets included. They prevent the water from boiling rapidly enough to cook pasta properly.

Serves 2-3 by itself or 4 with a steak; you can halve the recipe if serving a crowd of 2

2 lbs.	Manila clams	900 g
4 Tbsp.	olive oil	60 mL
3	cloves garlic, minced	3
2 Tbsp.	fresh parsley, finely chopped	30 mL
1	dried hot chili pepper, crumbled	1
1/2 cup	dry white wine	120 mL
1 lb.	dried linguine	454 g
2 Tbsp.	unsalted butter	30 mL
1/4 cup	freshly grated Parmesan cheese	60 mL

Wash the clams thoroughly, discarding any that do not close. Place them in a large pot, cover with a lid and steam over high heat until they open, shaking the pot to redistribute them. Remove the clams with a slotted spoon into a strainer over a bowl. Line a sieve with a double layer of paper towels and strain the juice from the pot and the juice from the draining clams. Reserve.

Remove the clams from their shells and chop coarsely. Place in a bowl and cover until ready to use.

In a heavy-bottomed pot, heat the olive oil over medium heat. Add the garlic and sauté until it just turns golden. Add the parsley, chili pepper and wine and let it boil away for a minute. Add the strained clam juice and boil for 1 minute longer. Remove from the heat.

Bring a large pot of water to a boil. Add the linguine to the boiling water and salt liberally. It should taste like seawater. Cook, stirring occasionally, until the pasta is very firm to the bite, about 8 minutes. Drain the pasta and return to the cooking pot. Add the clam juice mixture, the reserved clams and the butter. Stir over medium heat until piping hot and the pasta has reached its desired state of tenderness, 1-2 minutes. Stir in the Parmesan cheese. Serve immediately in heated bowls or alongside steaks.

Baked Halibut with Lemon, Tahini and Pine Nuts

This is an interpretation of a dish we used to eat in a small Middle Eastern café that also made excellent falafels. They used sole, and cod or snapper would be a good choice too. Serve with pita bread and Chopped Summer Salad with Mint and Parmesan Dressing, page 90, or Lebanese Bread Salad, page 89. This is great for a buffet.

Serves 6

2 lbs.	halibut filets	900 g
1/2 tsp.	salt	2.5 mL
1/2 tsp.	pepper	2.5 mL
	pinch of cayenne	
2 Tbsp.	lemon juice	30 mL
3 Tbsp.	olive oil	45 mL
2	onions, thinly sliced into half-moons	2
1/2 cup	tahini	120 mL
2	cloves garlic, crushed to a paste with 1/2 tsp. (2.5 mL) salt	2
1/2 cup	lemon juice	120 mL
1/2 cup	cold water	120 mL
2 Tbsp.	pine nuts	30 mL
1 Tbsp.	fresh parsley, coarsely chopped	15 mL

Cut the fish into 2-inch (5-cm) chunks and toss with the salt, pepper, cayenne and 2 Tbsp. (30 mL) lemon juice. Cover and refrigerate for 1 hour.

In a large, preferably nonstick frying pan, heat the olive oil over medium-low heat. Add the onion and cook until soft and a deep golden brown, about 15 minutes. Remove from the heat and set aside to drain on absorbent paper.

Place the tahini in a bowl. Slowly whisk in the garlic paste, lemon juice and water until smooth and creamy. Set aside.

Preheat the oven to 375°F (190°C). Lightly oil a baking dish that will hold the fish in one layer. Place the fish in the dish, cover tightly with aluminum foil and bake for 10 minutes. Remove the foil and bake for 5-10 minutes longer, until the fish is just cooked through.

Spread the tahini sauce over the fish. Sprinkle with the onion, pine nuts and parsley. Serve warm or at room temperature.

Halibut with Warm Bean and Tomato Salad

You can use asparagus instead of beans for this handsome hot-weather dish. The halibut may be grilled if you don't want to turn on the oven. The warm salad is delicious with salmon and cod as well.

Serves 4

1/2 lb.	green beans, trimmed	227 g
1/2 lb.	yellow beans, trimmed	227 g
1 Tbsp.	olive oil	15 mL
4	6-oz. (170-g) halibut filets	4
	salt and pepper to taste	
4 tsp.	balsamic vinegar	20 mL
1 1/2 tsp.	sugar	7.5 mL
1/2 cup	red onion, thinly sliced	120 mL
3	ripe plum tomatoes, cut into 1/2-inch (1.2-cm) cubes	3
3 Tbsp.	fresh basil, coarsely chopped	45 mL
	salt and pepper to taste	

Bring a large pot of water to a boil and salt liberally. Add the beans and cook until they are tender-crisp, 3-5 minutes. Drain and cool under cold water. Pat dry.

Preheat the oven to 400°F (200°C). In a heavy, ovenproof frying pan, heat the olive oil over high heat. Season the halibut filets with salt and pepper and cook in the hot oil for about 3 minutes, until the bottom is browned. Place the pan in the oven and cook the fish until just opaque, about 8 minutes. Place the fish on a heated plate. Cover and keep warm.

Add the beans to the frying pan and sauté over medium heat until the beans are heated through. Add the balsamic vinegar and sugar and stir to combine. Stir in the onion, tomatoes and basil. Season with salt and pepper. Spoon the bean and tomato mixture around the halibut filets and serve immediately.

Baked Halibut with Lemon Basil Vinaigrette

The halibut may be cooked on the grill if you prefer. Try frying the capers (see Tomato, Olive and Blue Cheese Salad with Crispy Capers, page 86) for a different flavor and texture.

Serves 4

4	6-oz. (170-g) fresh halibut filets	4
	salt and pepper to taste	
2 Tbsp.	freshly squeezed lemon juice	30 mL
1/4 tsp.	salt	1.2 mL
	pepper to taste	
1 tsp.	grated lemon zest	5 mL
2	cloves garlic, cut in half	2
2 Tbsp.	olive oil	30 mL
3 Tbsp.	fresh basil leaves, thinly sliced	45 mL
1 Tbsp.	drained capers	15 mL

Preheat the oven to 350°F (175°C). Season the halibut filets with salt and pepper. Lightly oil a baking dish and lay the halibut in the dish, without overlapping. Bake for 15-18 minutes, until the fish is opaque all the way through.

While the fish is baking, make the vinaigrette. Combine the lemon juice, salt, pepper and lemon zest in a small bowl. Spear the garlic on the tines of a fork and use it to beat the lemon juice mixture. Beat in the olive oil, basil and capers. Place the halibut on heated plates, spoon the vinaigrette over it and serve.

Salmon Steaks with Garlic and Green Chilies

If you like spice and heat, this recipe is for you. It is an excellent marinade for swordfish, shark or marlin as well.

Serves 6

6	6-oz. (170-g) salmon steaks	6
2 Tbsp.	vegetable oil	30 mL
3 Tbsp.	lemon juice	45 mL
1	medium onion, peeled and chopped	1
1	whole head of garlic, peeled and chopped	1
1	1-inch (2.5-cm) piece fresh ginger, peeled and chopped	1
2	jalapeño chilies, chopped	2
1/2 tsp.	salt	2.5 mL
1 tsp.	turmeric	5 mL

In the work bowl of a blender or food processor, combine all the ingredients except the fish. Blend until a fine paste is formed. Scrape into a bowl.

Add the salmon steaks and mix well to coat the steaks on both sides. Cover and refrigerate for at least 2 hours.

Heat the barbecue or broiler to high. Place the salmon steaks on the grill or 4 inches (10 cm) away from the broiler element and grill 3-4 minutes on each side for medium, brushing with the marinade. Serve immediately.

Red Snapper "Escabeche" Style

Escabeche is a dish of fish filets, marinated with vinegar, chilies, onion and spices. I have made a less "pickled" version by using lime juice instead of vinegar and shortening the marination time. Serve with Potato and Grilled Corn Salad with Buttermilk Cilantro Dressing, page 88, for a cool and refreshing summer repast. Thin halibut filets may be used instead.

Serves 4

1 tsp.	whole coriander seeds	5 mL
1 tsp.	whole cumin seeds	5 mL
1/2 tsp.	whole black peppercorns	2.5 mL
1/3 tsp.	salt	1.7 mL
3 Tbsp.	fresh lime juice	45 mL
5 Tbsp.	olive oil	75 mL
1	jalapeño pepper, thinly sliced	1
1/2 cup	all-purpose flour	120 mL
	salt and pepper to taste	
	cayenne pepper to taste	
4	6-oz. (170-g) Pacific red snapper filets	4
4 Tbsp.	olive oil	60 mL
1/2 cup	red onion, finely diced	120 mL
1/4 cup	fresh cilantro leaves	60 mL

Heat a small frying pan over medium heat. Add the coriander, cumin and peppercorns. Roast, shaking the pan, until the seeds turn a shade darker. Cool and crush coarsely. Place the crushed seeds in a small bowl with the salt. Whisk in the lime juice, 5 Tbsp. (75 mL) olive oil and the jalapeño pepper. Set aside.

Mix the flour, salt, pepper and cayenne pepper together on a plate. Dip the fish filets in the flour, coating both sides. Heat the 4 Tbsp. (60 mL) olive oil in a large frying pan on medium heat and sauté the fish filets until golden brown on both sides, 3-4 minutes. Transfer the filets to absorbent paper to drain. Arrange the filets on a platter, pour the sauce over them and sprinkle with red onion. Let cool. Sprinkle with the cilantro leaves, cover and refrigerate for 1-24 hours.

Stir-Fried Prawns with Lemon Grass, Cilantro and Mint

This has a lovely balance of hot, sweet and sour. Toasted rice powder is used in northern Thai and Laotian meat and fish "salads." It binds the liquid ingredients to the solids—very ingenious and well suited to low-fat cooking. The prawns may be poached or grilled instead of stir-fried.

Toasted Rice Powder

To make toasted rice powder, place 1/2 cup (120 mL) glutinous or long grain rice (see page 15) in a heavy frying pan and roast over medium heat until dark brown. Cool and grind to a fine powder in a spice mill or coffee grinder.

Serves 4

1 1/2 lbs.	large prawns, peeled	680 g
1 tsp.	black pepper	5 mL
1 Tbsp.	fish sauce	15 mL
1/2 tsp.	minced garlic	2.5 mL
1 Tbsp.	vegetable oil	15 mL
4 Tbsp.	lime juice	60 mL
2 Tbsp.	fish sauce	30 mL
2 tsp.	sugar	10 mL
3 Tbsp.	fresh lemon grass, thinly sliced	45 mL
3/4 cup	fresh cilantro leaves, coarsely chopped	180 mL
1 cup	fresh mint leaves, coarsely chopped	240 mL
1/2 cup	onion, thinly sliced	120 mL
1	serrano chili, finely chopped	1
2 Tbsp.	toasted rice powder	30 mL

In a bowl, mix the prawns, 1 Tbsp. (15 mL) pepper, fish sauce and garlic. Heat the vegetable oil over high heat in a large frying pan or wok. Add the prawns and stir-fry until they are pink and cooked all the way through, about 3 minutes. Transfer to a bowl. Add the lime juice, 2 Tbsp. (30 mL) fish sauce and sugar and mix well. Toss with the remaining ingredients and serve immediately.

Flaming Prawns!

When they bought my first book, Pacific Passions, *many people would ask, "Are the flaming prawns in it?" "Next book," I would say. This is the next book and these are the flaming prawns, one of the most popular dishes at the Fish House in Stanley Park.*

Serves 4 as an appetizer, 2 as a main course

1 Tbsp.	olive oil	15 mL
1 tsp.	garlic, minced	5 mL
24	large prawns, peeled and deveined	24
1/2 cup	roasted sweet red peppers, coarsely chopped (see Roasting Peppers, page 98)	120 mL
1/2 cup	well-drained, canned Italian plum tomatoes, coarsely chopped	120 mL
1/2 cup	crumbled feta cheese	120 mL
1/4 cup	fresh basil leaves	60 mL
1 oz.	ouzo, in a shot glass or small glass	30 mL
1/2	lemon, seeds removed	1/2

In a large frying pan, heat the olive oil over high heat. Add the garlic, and when it sizzles, add the prawns and stir-fry until they turn pink. Add the roasted peppers and tomatoes and stir-fry until the prawns are cooked through.

While the prawns are cooking, heat a heavy, preferably cast iron, frying pan over high heat. Have a wooden board ready to place the frying pan on and the ouzo and lemon ready where you are going to flame the prawns.

Add the feta and basil to the prawns and stir to combine. Transfer the prawns to one side of the hot frying pan and place the pan on the board. Carry the board to the table and advise everyone to stay well back. Pour the ouzo into the empty side of the pan and ignite immediately with a long match. Squeeze the lemon over the prawns to douse the flames, then give the prawns a stir. If pyrotechnics are not your style, just add the ouzo to the prawns after they have finished cooking. This, however, lacks drama. Serve with pasta, rice or bread to mop up the juices.

Deadly and Delicious Barbecued Garlic Prawns

The garlic and pepper make these deadly and delicious. You can serve them as an appetizer. Remove the shells from the prawns if you prefer, or broil them instead of grilling.

Serves 4-6

1 cup	unsalted butter	240 mL
1/4 cup	minced garlic	60 mL
12	green onions, thinly sliced	12
2 cups	dry white wine	475 mL
6 Tbsp.	freshly squeezed lemon juice	90 mL
2 Tbsp.	coarsely cracked black pepper	30 mL
1 1/2 lbs.	large prawns, about 35	680 g
1/2 cup	fresh parsley, finely chopped	120 mL
	salt to taste	
1/2 cup	fine dry breadcrumbs	120 mL

Prepare about 20 bamboo skewers by soaking them in water for 30 minutes.

Melt the butter in a large pot over medium heat. Add the garlic and onion and cook for 3-4 minutes, until the onion is soft. Add the wine and simmer the mixture for 15 minutes, stirring occasionally. Remove from the heat and add the lemon juice and pepper. Cool.

Cut halfway through each prawn by cutting down the back, through the shell; devein if necessary, but do not peel. Stir the prawns and parsley into the garlic mixture. Cover and refrigerate for 6-8 hours.

Let the marinade come to room temperature and remove the prawns. Place in a bowl, season liberally with salt, and toss with the breadcrumbs. Skewer 2 shrimp lengthwise on each skewer. Transfer the remaining marinade to a pot and simmer over low heat until thickened, 10-12 minutes.

Preheat the barbecue to high. Grill the shrimp until pink and cooked through, turning once, about 3-4 minutes. Serve on heated plates with the warm marinade on the side.

Steamed Clams with Saffron, Tomatoes and Pancetta

These clams are just as delicious without the pancetta. Serve with lots of bread to soak up the delicious juices.

Serves 4

2 Tbsp.	olive oil	30 mL
4	cloves garlic, minced	4
4 Tbsp.	pancetta, finely diced	60 mL
2 Tbsp.	white wine or cider vinegar	30 mL
2 Tbsp.	white wine	30 mL
	large pinch of saffron	
16	ripe cherry tomatoes, cut in half	16
1 tsp.	coarsely crushed black pepper	5 mL
2 Tbsp.	fresh parsley, finely chopped	30 mL
3 lbs.	fresh Manila clams, scrubbed	1.4 kg

In a pot large enough to hold the clams, heat the olive oil over medium heat. Add the garlic and pancetta. When they begin to sizzle, add the vinegar, wine and saffron.

Remove from the heat and let stand until the saffron begins to release its color. Add the tomatoes, pepper, parsley and clams. Cover with a lid and cook over high heat, shaking the pot occasionally, until the clams open. Divide the clams among 4 bowls and serve immediately.

Basic Chicken Sauté with a Multitude of Peppers (and Variations)

Quick, easy and good-looking too. You can use one, two or three colors of peppers if all are not available. Serve with steamed new potatoes, pasta or rice.

Stock or Broth?

My husband was in our local supermarket seeking frozen chicken stock. He asked one of the clerks if such a thing was to be had and she replied, deadly serious, "What part of the chicken is that from?" He came home with canned, low-sodium chicken broth. Canned chicken broth is fine to use in place of chicken stock in stir-fries, sautés, soups and pasta sauces. If a dish has no other thickening agent, such as flour, cornstarch or potatoes, and requires reducing the liquids to thicken it, use homemade or a reliable frozen chicken stock. Canned broth will not thicken as it reduces, though its flavor will become concentrated. That is why low-sodium chicken broth is advised.

Serves 4

4	skinless, boneless chicken breast halves	4
	salt and pepper to taste	
	all-purpose flour	
3 Tbsp.	olive oil	45 mL
2	cloves garlic, minced	2
1/2	sweet red pepper, cored and cut into 1-inch (2.5-cm) squares	1/2
1/2	sweet yellow pepper, cored and cut into 1-inch (2.5-cm) squares	1/2
1/2	sweet orange pepper, cored and cut into 1-inch (2.5-cm) squares	1/2
1/2	sweet green pepper, cored and cut into 1-inch (2.5-cm) squares	1/2
1/4 cup	dry white wine	60 mL
1 cup	chicken stock	240 mL
	salt and pepper to taste	
2 Tbsp.	fresh parsley, basil or dill, coarsely chopped	30 mL

Season the chicken breasts with salt and pepper and quickly dredge them in the flour.

Heat half the olive oil in a large, preferably nonstick pan over medium-high heat. Add the chicken breasts and cook until they are golden brown on both sides, turning once. Remove the chicken to a plate.

Add the remaining olive oil, garlic and peppers to the pan and sauté for 2-3 minutes, until slightly softened. Add the chicken and any juices to the pan, and the white wine. When the wine comes to a boil, add the chicken stock. Turn down to a simmer and cook for 5 minutes, turning the chicken once, until the sauce is lightly thickened and the chicken is cooked through. Season with salt and pepper and stir in the chopped fresh herb of your choice.

Variations

Southwestern Style: Add 1 cup (240 mL) fresh or thawed frozen corn kernels while the chicken is simmering, use chopped fresh cilantro as the fresh herb and add fresh or dried chilies to taste. Serve with warm tortillas.

Asian Style: Substitute 1 tsp. (5 mL) each grated orange rind, 2 tsp. (10 mL) soy sauce, 1/2 tsp. (2.5 mL) sesame oil and 2 thinly sliced green onions for the fresh herbs before you remove the chicken from the heat. Serve with steamed rice.

Mediterranean Style: Add 1 tsp. (5 mL) grated lemon rind, 1/2 tsp. (2.5 mL) dried oregano, 1/4 cup (60 mL) crumbled feta cheese, 1/4 cup (60 mL) pitted black olives and use chopped parsley for the fresh herb before you remove the chicken from the heat. Serve with buttered orzo or saffron rice.

Chilled Corn and Chicken Soup with Tomato and Cilantro

A lovely, hot-weather main course, served with corn chips. For a very smooth-textured soup, you can strain the purée through a sieve. Press on the solids to extract all the liquid, then discard the solids.

Serves 4

1 lb.	boneless, skinless chicken breasts	454 g
7 cups	chicken stock	1.7 L
4	leeks, white part only, cleaned and finely sliced	4
1/2 lb.	large, new red potatoes, peeled and diced	227 g
4 cups	fresh or frozen corn kernels	950 mL
1 tsp.	whole cumin seeds	5 mL
1/4 tsp.	cayenne pepper	1.2 mL
	salt and pepper to taste	
1	medium ripe tomato, finely diced	1
1	avocado, peeled, pitted and finely diced	1
1 Tbsp.	fresh cilantro, coarsely chopped	15 mL
2 tsp.	lime juice	10 mL
	salt and pepper to taste	
1/2 cup	yogurt	120 mL

Place the chicken in a single layer in a pot or frying pan. Cover with chicken stock by 1 inch (2.5 cm). Bring to a simmer and cook 10 minutes. Remove from the heat and let stand, covered, until cool. Cover and refrigerate the chicken, reserving the stock.

In a large pot, combine the remaining chicken stock, reserved stock, leeks, potatoes, corn, cumin, cayenne, salt and pepper. Bring to a boil and simmer for 15-20 minutes, until the potatoes are very tender. In a blender or food processor, purée 2/3 of the soup in batches until smooth. Place the purée in a large bowl and add the remaining soup. Taste and correct the seasoning. Refrigerate the soup until cold or for up to 1 day.

Shred the cooked chicken. Combine the tomato, avocado, cilantro and lime juice. Season with salt and pepper.

Whisk the yogurt into the chilled soup. If the soup seems too thick, thin it with cold water. Taste and adjust the seasoning. Ladle the soup into bowls and top with the tomato mixture and the chicken.

Chopped Chicken Salad with Creamy Basil Dressing

Chopped salads, as the name suggests, incorporate a number of ingredients chopped into small, manageable pieces. With each forkful, you get a variety of textures and flavors. You can toss everything in a bowl or create rows of the components on top of the lettuce and then toss at the table. A perfect summer meal with a loaf of bread. Use cooked turkey instead of the chicken if you wish.

Serves 4

1/2 cup	mayonnaise	120 mL
1/4 cup	yogurt	60 mL
1 Tbsp.	lemon juice	15 mL
2 tsp.	Dijon mustard	10 mL
1/2 tsp.	salt	2.5 mL
1/2 cup	fresh basil, finely chopped	120 mL
1	clove garlic, minced	1
1	large head romaine lettuce, washed, dried and cut into 1/2-inch (1.2-cm) squares	1
1 cup	cucumber, peeled, seeded and cut into 1/2-inch (1.2-cm) cubes	240 mL
1 1/2 cups	tomatoes, cut into 1/2-inch (1.2-cm) cubes	360 mL
2	green onions, thinly sliced	2
1/2 cup	celery hearts, cut into 1/2-inch (1.2-cm) squares	120 mL
1 cup	tart apple, diced into 1/2-inch (1.2-cm) cubes and tossed with 1 Tbsp. (15 mL) lemon juice	240 mL
3 cups	cooked chicken, cut into 1/2-inch (1.2-cm) cubes	720 mL
1 cup	grated asiago cheese	240 mL

Stir the mayonnaise, yogurt, lemon juice, Dijon mustard, salt, basil and garlic together. Refrigerate for 1 hour to develop the flavors.

Place the lettuce in a serving bowl and arrange the remaining ingredients in rows, spokes or willy-nilly over the lettuce. Pour the dressing over the salad and toss well.

Turkey Tenderloins with Roasted Sweet Red Pepper and Garlic Sauce

You can substitute pork tenderloin or chicken for the turkey and grill or broil the meat instead of pan-roasting it. The recipe can be easily halved.

Serves 6-8

1/2 cup	olive oil	120 mL
6	cloves garlic, minced	6
1/2 tsp.	salt	2.5 mL
1/2 tsp.	pepper	2.5
1 Tbsp.	freshly squeezed lemon juice	15 mL
2 tsp.	fresh thyme leaves	10 mL
1 Tbsp.	fresh parsley, finely chopped	15 mL
4	turkey tenderloins, about 3 lbs. (1.4 kg) in total	4

In a large bowl, combine the olive oil, garlic, salt, pepper, lemon juice, thyme and parsley. Add the tenderloins and stir well to coat. Cover and refrigerate for 1-24 hours.

Preheat the oven to 350°F (175°C). Heat a large, oven-proof, preferably nonstick frying pan over medium heat. Add the tenderloins and cook until browned on both sides, 2-3 minutes per side. Place the pan in the oven and bake until the tenderloins are cooked through, 10-12 minutes. Remove from the oven and let stand for a few minutes before slicing. Serve the sauce on the side.

Roasted Sweet Red Pepper and Garlic Sauce

This sauce is great with chicken and pork or drizzled on a vegetable salad or pasta.

Makes about 2 1/2 cups (600 mL)

6	sweet red peppers, roasted, peeled and seeded (see Roasting Peppers, page 98)	6
6	cloves garlic, minced	6
1/2 tsp.	salt	2.5 mL
1/4 cup	sliced almonds	60 mL
1/2 cup	soft white breadcrumbs	120 mL
1/4 tsp.	cayenne pepper	1.2 mL
1/2 cup	olive oil	120 mL
1 Tbsp.	lemon juice	15 mL

Drain the roasted peppers in a sieve for 1/2 hour. Place the peppers, garlic, salt, almonds, breadcrumbs, and cayenne in a blender or food processor and purée until smooth. With the motor running, slowly add the olive oil and lemon juice. Taste and adjust the seasoning. Cover and refrigerate. Keeps for 5 days.

Graham's Grilled Flank Steak with Cumin Aioli

Co-worker Graham raved about a steak salad with cumin aioli. It was served in a restaurant he used to work in and he often made it at home. His ravings got my wheels turning and out came this interpretation. Serve it with a green salad or Chopped Summer Salad with Mint and Parmesan Dressing, page 90. You can use a sirloin steak in place of the flank steak.

Serves 4

3 Tbsp.	oyster sauce	45 mL
2	cloves garlic, minced	2
1/2 tsp.	coarsely ground black pepper	2.5 mL
1	flank steak, about 2 1/2 lbs. (1.1 kg)	1
1 Tbsp.	cumin seeds	15 mL
1	large egg	1
1 tsp.	Dijon mustard	5 mL
1/2 tsp.	salt	2.5 mL
1	clove garlic, minced	1
1/2 cup	vegetable oil	120 mL
1/2 cup	olive oil	120 mL
4 tsp.	lemon juice	20 mL

Mix the oyster sauce, garlic and black pepper together in a small bowl. Spread on both sides of the steak. Cover and refrigerate.

Dry-roast the cumin seeds in a small frying pan over medium heat until they darken a shade. Remove from the heat. Finely grind half of the cumin seeds in a spice or coffee grinder. In a blender or food processor, combine the egg, mustard, salt, garlic and the finely ground cumin seeds. With the motor on, add half of the oils in a slow steady stream. Add the lemon juice and continue adding the rest of the oil until the aioli is emulsified. If it seems too thick, add a spoonful or two of water. Scrape the aioli into a bowl and stir in the whole cumin seeds.

Preheat the barbecue or broiler to high. Grill or broil the steak 3-4 minutes on each side for medium-rare. Remove the steak from the heat and let it rest for a few minutes. Slice very thinly across the grain and serve with the cumin aioli on the side.

Note: If using raw egg makes you uncomfortable, substitute 1 cup (240 mL) prepared mayonnaise for the egg, salt, oil and lemon juice. Stir the ground and whole cumin seeds, mustard and garlic into the mayonnaise.

Tomato, Olive and Blue Cheese Salad with Crispy Capers

Another great way to utilize summer tomatoes.

Serves 6

1 Tbsp.	vegetable oil	15 mL
2 Tbsp.	drained capers, patted dry with absorbent paper	30 mL
6	large, ripe tomatoes	6
2 Tbsp.	balsamic vinegar	30 mL
1/3 tsp.	salt	1.7 mL
1 Tbsp.	shallots, finely chopped	15 mL
5 Tbsp.	olive oil	75 mL
1/2 cup	pitted black olives, cut in half	120 mL
1/3 cup	blue cheese, crumbled	80 mL

Heat the vegetable oil in a small, preferably nonstick frying pan over high heat. Add the capers and fry, shaking the pan until the capers turn a shade lighter. Drain the capers through a sieve and lay them out on absorbent paper.

Cut the tomatoes into thick slices and arrange on a platter. Whisk the vinegar, salt and shallots together. Whisk in the olive oil. Drizzle the dressing over the tomatoes. Scatter the olives, blue cheese and capers over the salad. Serve immediately.

Tomato and Potato Salad with Cucumber and Feta Dressing

Serves 4

This is a good warm-weather main course. Serve with a plate of olives, roasted red peppers, hot pickled peppers and pita bread.

2	large red potatoes, a scant pound (450 g)	2
1 cup	cucumber, peeled, seeded and grated	240 mL
1/4 cup	crumbled feta cheese	60 mL
1/2 cup	yogurt	120 mL
1	clove garlic, minced	1
1/4 tsp.	salt	1.2 mL
	large pinch of black pepper	
2	large ripe tomatoes	2
2 Tbsp.	fresh dill, coarsely chopped	30 mL

Place the potatoes in a pot and cover with cold water by 2 inches (5 cm). Bring to a boil and cook until the potatoes are tender when pierced with a knife, 20-25 minutes. Drain and cool. Refrigerate until cold.

Using your hands, squeeze the water out of the grated cucumber. Place in a blender or food processor with the feta, yogurt, garlic, salt and pepper. Purée until smooth. Cover and refrigerate.

Cut the potatoes and tomatoes into 1/4-inch (.6-cm) slices and arrange on a large plate or platter, overlapping them. Drizzle with the cucumber dressing and sprinkle with the chopped dill.

Potato and Grilled Corn Salad with Buttermilk Cilantro Dressing

Serves 6-8

Serve with salmon, crab, lobster or a Southwestern-inspired meal.

3 lbs.	red potatoes	1.4 kg
3 cobs	fresh corn, husked	3 cobs
1 Tbsp.	olive oil	15 mL
	salt and pepper to taste	
1/2 cup	sweet red pepper, finely diced	120 mL
1/2 cup	buttermilk	120 mL
1/2 cup	mayonnaise	120 mL
4 tsp.	lime juice	20 mL
1/2 tsp.	salt	2.5 mL
	large pinch of cayenne	
1/2 tsp.	paprika	2.5 mL
2	green onions, thinly sliced	2
2 Tbsp.	fresh cilantro, coarsely chopped	30 mL

Cut the potatoes into 1-inch (2.5-cm) cubes. Place in a pot and cover with cold salted water by a few inches (10 cm). Bring to a boil and cook the potatoes until they are tender, 10-15 minutes. Drain and cool. Place in a large bowl.

Preheat the barbecue to high. Brush the corn with the olive oil and season with salt and pepper. Grill the corn, turning as it becomes speckled with brown. Remove from the heat and cool. Cut the corn from the cobs and add to the potatoes. Add the sweet red pepper.

Combine the buttermilk, mayonnaise, lime juice, salt, cayenne, paprika, onion and cilantro until well blended. Pour over the vegetables and mix well. Serve immediately or cover and refrigerate for up to 24 hours.

Lebanese Bread Salad

I was taught how to make this salad many moons ago, in Ottawa. It traditionally has a spice mixture called za'atar added to it, made of sumac, thyme and sesame seeds. If you know of a store that sells Middle Eastern foods, obtain some za'atar and add a few spoonfuls to the salad. It is also delicious eaten with bread that has been dipped in olive oil.

Serves 6-8

1	small sweet green or red pepper, cored and cut into 1/2-inch (1.2-cm) dice	1
1/3	English cucumber, cut into 1/2-inch (1.2-cm) dice	1/3
1 cup	green onion, thinly sliced	240 mL
1 1/2 cups	fresh parsley, coarsely chopped	360 mL
1/4 cup	fresh mint leaves, coarsely chopped	60 mL
2	cloves garlic, minced and crushed to a paste with 1/2 tsp. (2.5 mL) salt	2
1/4 cup	lemon juice	60 mL
1/2 cup	olive oil	120 mL
1	large pinch ground cinnamon	1
1	large pinch ground allspice	1
	salt to taste	
3	medium, ripe tomatoes, cut into 1/2-inch (1.2-cm) dice	3
4	small pita breads, separated into halves, lightly toasted and broken into 1/2-inch (1.2-cm) pieces	4

In a large bowl, combine the pepper, cucumber, green onion, parsley and mint. Mix together the garlic paste, lemon juice, olive oil, cinnamon and allspice. Set aside.

When ready to serve, toss the salad with the dressing. Check for salt. Add the tomatoes and pita and toss again.

Chopped Summer Salad with Mint and Parmesan Dressing

This salad is good with any simply prepared meat, fish or fowl. Try it with Graham's Grilled Flank Steak with Cumin Aioli, page 85.

Serves 4-6

1	clove garlic, minced	1
1/2 tsp.	salt	2.5 mL
2 tsp.	Dijon mustard	10 mL
1 Tbsp.	white wine vinegar	15 mL
5 Tbsp.	vegetable oil	75 mL
3 Tbsp.	olive oil	45 mL
1 1/2 cups	peeled, seeded cucumber, diced into 1/2-inch (1.2-cm) cubes	360 mL
1	head of romaine lettuce, washed, dried and cut into 1/2-inch (1.2-cm) squares	1
1 cup	radishes, diced into 1/2-inch (1.2-cm) cubes	240 mL
2 cups	tomatoes, diced into 1/2-inch (1.2-cm) cubes	475 mL
1 cup	yellow pepper, cut into 1/2-inch (1.2-cm) squares	240 mL
1/4 cup	finely diced red onion	60 mL
1/2 cup	freshly grated Parmesan cheese	120 mL
1/2 cup	fresh mint, coarsely chopped	120 mL

In a small bowl, whisk the garlic, salt, Dijon mustard and vinegar together. Slowly whisk in the vegetable and olive oils.

Mix all the vegetables together in a large bowl. Pour the dressing over the vegetables and toss well. Add the Parmesan cheese and mint and toss again.

Caponata

A Toronto supplier of excellent wines and olive oils gave me a jar filled with a miraculous eggplant dish that his mother made. It was a perfect blend of sweet, sour and salty, with a creamy texture. I was so impressed that I immediately set to work replicating it and it seemed like that's all we ate that summer—on pasta, with meat and fish, on salads, with cheese, as an appetizer. We fed it to our friends. They started making it. And so on…This is one of my favorite dishes of all time. If you can find the Sicilian eggplants that appear in the summer, use them. They are the sweetest.

Makes about 2 cups (475 mL)

1 lb.	eggplant	454 g
1/4 cup	olive oil	60 mL
1 stalk	celery, cut into julienne strips, 2 inches by 1/4 inch (5 cm by .6 cm)	1
1	medium onion, cut into 1/2-inch (1.2-cm) lengthwise wedges	1
1 1/2 cups	drained, canned plum tomatoes, puréed and sieved	360 mL
8	good-quality green olives, pitted	8
8	good-quality black olives, pitted	8
1 Tbsp.	small capers, drained	15 mL
1 1/2 tsp.	golden raisins	7.5 mL
	salt and black pepper to taste	
1 tsp.	balsamic vinegar	5 mL
1 1/2 tsp.	fresh Italian parsley, coarsely chopped	7.5 mL
1/2 cup	fresh basil leaves	120 mL

Preheat the oven to 350°F (175°C). Prick the eggplant several times with a fork and place on a baking sheet. Bake for 30-45 minutes, until the eggplant is completely soft and collapsing. Remove from the oven and slit the eggplant open on one side. Place in a colander, slit side down, to drain and cool completely.

While the eggplant is cooling, heat the olive oil in a large pot over medium heat. Add the celery and onion and sauté until translucent. Add the tomato purée, olives, capers and raisins. Cook over medium heat for about 10 minutes, stirring occasionally, until it is slightly thickened and the oil starts to separate from the tomato mixture.

When the eggplant has cooled, peel off the skin. Chop the eggplant crosswise into 2-inch (5-cm) pieces. Add to the tomato mixture and simmer for 10 minutes. Season with salt and pepper. Add the balsamic vinegar, parsley and basil and remove from the heat. Keeps for a week in the refrigerator.

Roasted Summer Tomatoes with Parsley, Garlic and Olive Oil

These look so good when cooked it is hard to resist eating them out of the pan! Great hot, cold or at room temperature.

Serves 6-8

2 lbs.	perfectly ripe tomatoes, about 8	900 g
1/2 tsp	salt	2.5 mL
4 Tbsp.	olive oil	60 mL
4	cloves garlic, minced	4
2 Tbsp.	fresh parsley, finely chopped	30 mL
1 tsp.	ground black pepper	5 mL

Preheat the oven to 400°F (200°C). Wash and cut the tomatoes in half crosswise. Place them, cut side up, in a 9- by 13-inch (23- by 33-cm) baking dish. They will fit snugly. Sprinkle with the salt and drizzle with 2 Tbsp. (30 mL) of the olive oil. Place on the middle rack of the oven and bake for 45 minutes. Mix together the remaining olive oil, garlic, parsley and black pepper. Remove the tomatoes from the oven and spread with the mixture. Return to the oven and bake 45 minutes longer.

Grilled Eggplant Salad with Honey and Mint

The creaminess of the eggplant works brilliantly with the sweet and sour flavor of the honey and lemon.

Serves 6

3 lbs.	small firm eggplants	1.4 kg
1	small clove garlic	1
1/2 tsp.	salt	2.5 mL
1 Tbsp.	honey	15 mL
2 Tbsp.	lemon juice	30 mL
6 Tbsp.	olive oil	90 mL
2-3 Tbsp.	fresh mint, shredded	30-45 mL
1 Tbsp.	fresh parsley, chopped	15 mL

Remove the stem and bottom from the eggplant and slice into 1-inch-thick (2.5-cm) slices. Brush lightly on both sides with olive oil and grill or broil on both sides until browned and tender. Transfer the slices to a shallow serving dish, overlapping them slightly.

Crush the garlic to a paste with the salt. Whisk it together with the honey, lemon juice and olive oil. Drizzle over the eggplant. Serve immediately or cover with plastic wrap and let stand until ready to serve. Just before serving, sprinkle with the mint and parsley. The salad can be made the day before but remove from the fridge well in advance, as it is best served at room temperature.

Corn Pancakes

If you omit the green onion, these are great for breakfast with a downpour of maple syrup. Made with onions, they can be eaten with almost any saucy meat, fish or vegetables.

Makes about 18 small pancakes

3/4 cup	all-purpose flour	180 mL
1/2 cup	yellow cornmeal	120 mL
1/2 tsp.	baking powder	2.5 mL
1/2 tsp.	baking soda	2.5 mL
1 tsp.	salt	5 mL
2 tsp.	sugar	10 mL
1 1/4 cups	buttermilk	300 mL
2 Tbsp.	unsalted butter, melted and cooled	30 mL
1	egg, beaten	1
1 cup	corn kernels, fresh or thawed if frozen	240 mL
2	green onions, finely chopped	2

With a whisk, combine the flour, cornmeal, baking powder and soda, salt and sugar. In a large bowl, whisk the buttermilk, unsalted butter and egg together. Add the dry ingredients and fold into the wet ingredients. Gently stir in the corn and green onion.

Heat a nonstick or lightly oiled heavy frying pan over medium heat. Ladle a scant 1/4 cup (60 mL) into the pan for each pancake. Cook until bubbles appear around the edge of the pancakes. Flip over and cook until golden brown. Keep warm in a 250°F (120°C) oven while preparing the remaining pancakes.

Fresh Corn Pudding

*Corn, cream and eggs,
pure and simple. You
can use the fancy
presentation described
here or just serve it
plain. I have an
attachment to simple
corn dishes—
pancakes, fritters,
spoon bread served
with a drizzle of
maple syrup. Serve
it for brunch with
bacon or sausages.
Dee-licious!*

Serves 4-6

6	large ears fresh corn	6
1 cup	whipping cream or milk	240 mL
3	large eggs at room temperature, separated	3
2 Tbsp.	unsalted butter, melted	30 mL
1 Tbsp.	sugar	15 mL
3/4 tsp.	salt	4 mL
	pinch of cayenne pepper	

Husk the corn and remove all the silk. Reserve 20 of the
nice inner husks. Stack them up, and place a baking sheet
over them. Place a weight on top of the baking sheet and
let stand for 1/2 hour. You are flattening the cornhusks to
line the baking dish.

Preheat the oven to 350°F (175°C). Butter an 8-inch-
square (20-cm) glass baking dish. Position one of the
husks with the pointed end a few inches (8 cm) above the
rim of the dish and the blunt end toward the center. Press
the husk along the side of the dish and across the bottom.
Continue along the side of the dish, slightly overlapping
the cornhusks. Do the same on the opposite side. You may
not need all the husks. This step may be omitted if you
prefer.

Slice the corn kernels from each cob into a bowl. Scrape
along each cob to extract any juices. Whisk in the cream
or milk, egg yolks, butter, sugar, salt and cayenne. In a
separate bowl, beat the egg whites until stiff but not dry.
Fold into the corn mixture. Pour the batter into the
prepared pan. Place the baking dish in a larger pan and
pour enough hot water into the outer pan so that it comes
halfway up the side of the baking dish. Bake for 25-30
minutes, until barely set in the middle. Serve either hot or
warm.

"Dry Roasted" Szechuan Green Beans

One of my favorite stir-fries in the Chinese repertoire is this savory dish of green beans cooked with chilies and ground beef. I can eat it hot or cold, with rice or without. Normally, the green beans are deep-fried before being stir-fried—a process that gives them a chewy, supple texture but makes them extremely oily. A light coating of oil and roasting the beans at a high temperature mimics the texture of the deep-fried beans. Be warned, the beans are not pretty when they come from the oven, but it is hard to resist eating them from the pan.

Serves 2 as a main course

1 1/2 lbs.	green beans, trimmed	680 g
2 Tbsp.	vegetable oil	30 mL
1/4 tsp.	salt	1.2 mL
2 Tbsp.	ginger root, finely chopped	30 mL
4	cloves garlic, minced	4
1	jalapeño or serrano chili, finely chopped	1
2	green onions, white part only, thinly sliced	2
1/4 lb.	lean ground beef	113 g
3 Tbsp.	light soy sauce	45 mL
1 Tbsp.	Chinese cooking wine	15 mL
1 tsp.	sugar	5 mL
1/2 cup	chicken stock or water	120 mL
1 tsp.	cornstarch	5 mL

Preheat the oven to 500°F (260°C).

Place a heavy baking sheet with a rim in the oven and heat for 10 minutes. Toss the beans with 1 Tbsp. (15 mL) of the vegetable oil and the salt. Remove the baking sheet from the oven and quickly spread the beans out in as even a layer as possible. Bake for 5 minutes. Turn the beans over, spread them out again and bake for another 5 minutes. Repeat the procedure one more time and remove from the oven.

Heat a wok or large frying pan over high heat until just smoking. Add the remaining vegetable oil, ginger, garlic, chili pepper and green onion. Stir-fry for a few moments to release the fragrance of the ginger. Add the beef, crumbling it with the back of a spoon until it is well cooked, about 2 minutes. Add the green beans, stir once or twice, and add the soy sauce, cooking wine and sugar. Stir-fry until the liquid comes to a boil and reduces slightly. Mix the stock or water with the cornstarch, add it to the mixture and cook until the liquid thickens. Serve immediately.

Fusilli with Zucchini and Lemon

You can add fresh basil, parsley or mint to this pasta if you like.

Serves 4

2 Tbsp.	olive oil	30 mL
4	medium zucchini, cut into 2- by 1/2-inch (5- by 1.2-cm) sticks	4
1 Tbsp.	unsalted butter	15 mL
2	cloves garlic, minced	2
1/2 cup	dry white wine	120 mL
1 cup	chicken stock	240 mL
1/2 cup	whipping cream or half-and-half cream	120 mL
2 tsp.	lemon zest	10 mL
	salt and pepper to taste	
1 lb.	dry fusilli	454 g
1/4 cup	freshly grated Parmesan cheese	60 mL

Heat the olive oil over high heat in a large, heavy frying pan. Add the zucchini in a single layer, in batches if necessary, and fry until it is browned on the bottom. Transfer to a plate.

Melt the butter over medium heat in a large pot. Add the garlic and sauté for a minute. Add the white wine and chicken stock and reduce by half over high heat. Add the whipping cream and boil until slightly thickened. Add the lemon zest and season with salt and pepper.

Bring a large pot of water to a boil. Add the fusilli to the boiling water and salt liberally. It should taste like seawater. Cook, stirring occasionally, until the pasta is tender but still firm to the bite, 8-10 minutes. Drain and return the pasta to the cooking pot. Add the sauce and zucchini and stir over high heat until piping hot. Stir in the Parmesan cheese. Serve immediately in heated bowls.

Corn and Basmati Rice Pilaf

Make this fragrant pilaf as a change from plain rice.

Serves 4 as a side dish

1 cup	basmati rice	240 mL
1 Tbsp.	vegetable oil	15 mL
1/2 tsp.	cumin seeds	2.5 mL
4	whole green cardamom pods	4
1	2-inch (5-cm) cinnamon stick	1
2 1/4 cups	water or chicken stock	535 mL
3/4 cup	fresh or frozen corn kernels, thawed	180 mL
	salt and pepper to taste	

Wash the rice by placing it in a bowl, covering with water, and swishing the rice around with your hand. Pour off the water and continue washing until the water runs clear. Drain in a sieve and let sit for 1/2 hour.

Heat the oil in a medium-sized, heavy pot over medium-high heat. Add the cumin seeds, cardamom pods and cinnamon stick. Sauté until the cumin darkens a shade, about 1 minute. Add the rice and stir to coat with the oil. Add the water or stock and bring to a boil. Reduce the heat to low, add the corn, cover tightly, and cook until the rice is tender, 15-20 minutes. Remove the rice from the heat and let rest for 5 minutes, covered. Fluff with a fork and season to taste.

Sweet Red Pepper "Vichyssoise"

A lovely salmon-pink color, this can be served hot or cold.

Roasting Peppers

If you have a gas stove, turn a burner on high and place the pepper directly on the flame. Turn the pepper with tongs to blacken the skin on all sides. On an electric stove, preheat the broiler to high. Place the peppers on a baking sheet as close to the element as possible. Turn the peppers with tongs to blacken the skin on all sides. Cool, slip off the skins and remove the seeds and core.

Serves 6

1 Tbsp.	unsalted butter	15 mL
4	large leeks, white part only, cleaned and thinly sliced (see A Bit About Leeks, page 191)	4
1	medium onion, thinly sliced	1
1 lb.	russet potatoes, peeled and thickly sliced	454 g
5 cups	chicken stock	1.2 L
	salt to taste	
1 lb.	sweet red peppers, roasted, seeded and peeled	454 g
2 cups	milk	475 mL
2 cups	half-and-half cream or milk	475 mL
1 cup	sour cream	240 mL
2 Tbsp.	freshly squeezed lemon juice	30 mL

Melt the butter over medium heat in a large pot. Add the leeks and onion and sauté until soft but not brown. Add the potatoes, chicken stock and salt. Turn down to a simmer and cook, partially covered, until the potatoes are very tender, 20-30 minutes. Add all the roasted sweet red peppers except one.

In batches, purée the soup in a blender or food processor, then strain through a sieve to make it perfectly smooth. Return it to the pot, add the milk and cream and bring to a boil. Finely chop the reserved sweet red pepper and add it to the soup. Remove from the heat and stir in the sour cream and lemon juice. If you want to serve it cold, add the sour cream and lemon juice after the soup has chilled for 2-24 hours. Adjust the seasoning and serve.

Watermelon Granita

A granita is a simply made frozen dessert, usually fruit-based, that requires no special freezing equipment. The better the fruit, the better your granita will be, so use only summer-ripened, juicy watermelons.

Serves 6

1/3 cup	sugar	80 mL
1/3 cup	water	80 mL
2 Tbsp.	fresh lime juice	30 mL
2 Tbsp.	vodka	30 mL
5 cups	seedless watermelon, cut into 1-inch (2.5-cm) cubes	1.2 L

In a small pot, combine the sugar and water. Bring to a boil, stirring until the sugar dissolves. Remove from the heat and cool. Stir in the lime juice and vodka. Place half the sugar mixture and half the watermelon cubes in a blender or food processor. Purée until smooth and pour into a 9- by 13-inch (23- by 33-cm) glass baking dish. Repeat with the remaining ingredients. Freeze for 3 hours, stirring with a whisk every 30 minutes until it is completely frozen into small granules. It will keep frozen for up to 2 days. Stir with a fork before serving.

Strawberries Steeped in Port with Mascarpone and Honey Cream

Experiment with this recipe and use your favorite sweet dessert wine. Dessert wines made from muscat grapes are some of my favorites.

Serves 4

2 pints	strawberries	950 mL
1/4 cup	port	60 mL
3 Tbsp.	sugar	45 mL
1/4 cup	mascarpone cheese	60 mL
2 Tbsp.	liquid honey	30 mL
1/2 cup	whipping cream, softly whipped	120 mL

Quickly wash the strawberries and dry by setting them on paper towels. Hull and cut the berries into quarters. Transfer to a bowl and add the port and sugar. Stir gently to combine and let sit at room temperature for 1/2 hour. Whisk the mascarpone with the honey until smooth and fold in the whipped cream. Spoon the berries into four wine glasses and garnish with the mascarpone cream.

Fresh Berries with Champagne Sabayon

Sabayon is a relative of the Italian zabaglione, a warm dessert of whipped egg yolks, sugar and marsala. We have served it over cassis sorbet for a "frozen" Kir Royale. Use any combination of summer fruits or berries.

Serves 6

6	large egg yolks	6
10 Tbsp.	sugar	150 mL
6 Tbsp.	dry champagne or sparkling wine	90 mL
1 cup	whipping cream	240 mL
1 pint	raspberries	475 mL
1 pint	strawberries	475 mL

With a whisk, beat the egg yolks and sugar together in a heatproof bowl. Place the bowl over a pot of simmering water without letting the bottom of the bowl touch the water. Whisk until thick and increased in volume, 6-8 minutes. Remove from the pot and whisk in the champagne. Place the bowl in a larger bowl of ice and let stand until cool, whisking occasionally. Cover and refrigerate.

When you are ready to serve, whip the cream into soft peaks and fold into the champagne mixture. Divide the berries among 6 wine glasses and top with the sabayon.

Summer Melon and Red Currants in Sweet Wine

One of the bonuses of living in British Columbia is enjoying the spectacular dessert wines produced here. Riesling and Ehrenfelser are popular. Other than drinking them, they can be used to their best advantage in simple desserts. Look for local melons that are fragrant, very sweet and slightly soft at the stem end. Try to choose two colors of melon for maximum visual effect. A perfect ending for a midsummer dinner.

Serves 4-6

2 lbs.	sweet, fragrant melons	900 g
1 pint	fresh red currants	475 mL
2 Tbsp.	sugar	30 mL
1/2 cup	dessert wine	120 mL

Cut the melons in half, remove the seeds and peel. Dice the melons into 1/2-inch (1.2-cm) pieces and place in a bowl.

Quickly wash the red currants and set them out on towels to dry. Remove the stems, being careful not to crush the currants. Save several clusters to garnish the finished dish. Add the red currants to the melon. The fruit may be prepared up to 2 hours in advance. Cover and refrigerate.

When you are ready to serve the dessert, pour the sweet wine and sugar over the fruit and stir gently to combine. Transfer to a serving dish and garnish with currant clusters.

Fresh Pineapple with Lemon Grass and Ginger Syrup

Eat this as is for a low-fat dessert or add a scoop of vanilla ice cream. The syrup makes a good base for fruit salads. Cantaloupe and strawberry is a particularly good combination.

Serves 6

1/2 cup	sugar	120 mL
20	quarter-sized slices of fresh peeled ginger	20
2	stalks lemon grass, trimmed and coarse leaves discarded, cut into 2-inch (5-cm) lengths	2
1 cup	water	240 mL
1/4 cup	sweet white dessert wine	60 mL
1	large, ripe pineapple	1
1 Tbsp.	fresh mint, coarsely chopped	15 mL

In a small noncorrodible pot, combine the sugar, ginger, lemon grass, water and dessert wine. Bring to a boil over high heat and boil until reduced to 2/3 cup (160 mL), about 5 minutes. Remove from the heat and cool.

Peel the pineapple. Quarter lengthwise, core and cut into 1/2-inch (1.2-cm) slices. Add the syrup to the pineapple and mix well. Refrigerate for up to 24 hours.

Spoon into wine glasses if desired. Sprinkle with mint and serve.

Sour Cherry Cobbler

Sour cherries are one of summer's treats. This is an excellent way of using them. Serve with rum-flavored whipped cream.

Serves 6

4 cups	sour cherries, pitted	950 ml
3/4 cup	sugar	180 ml
3 Tbsp.	cornstarch	45 ml
2 Tbsp.	water	30 ml
1/2 tsp.	ground cinnamon	2.5 ml
1/4 tsp.	ground nutmeg	1.2 ml
2 Tbsp.	unsalted butter	30 ml
1 cup	all-purpose flour	240 ml
1/2 cup	sugar	120 ml
1 1/2 tsp.	baking powder	7.5 ml
1/2 tsp.	salt	2.5 ml
2 Tbsp.	unsalted butter, chilled	30 ml
2/3 cup	whipping cream	160 ml

Preheat the oven to 400°F (200°C). In a large pot, combine the sour cherries and sugar. Cook over low heat until the juice starts to flow from the cherries. Mix the cornstarch and water. Add to the cherries, stirring constantly, and increase the heat to high. Cook until the mixture is thick and bubbly. Stir in the cinnamon, nutmeg and butter and transfer to a 9-inch (23-cm) baking dish.

Combine the flour, sugar, baking powder and salt in a medium bowl. Cut the chilled butter into the flour until a coarse meal forms. Stir in the whipping cream to form a soft dough. Roll out on a lightly floured surface to a 6-inch (15-cm) square. Cut the dough into 12 rectangles and arrange on top of the cherries. Bake in the middle of the oven until the biscuits are puffed and golden, about 30 minutes. Cool slightly before serving.

Blueberry Sour Cream Pie

You can substitute Crème Fraîche, page 205, for the sour cream if you like.

Serves 8
The crust:

1 1/4 cups	all-purpose flour	300 mL
2 Tbsp.	sugar	30 mL
	pinch of salt	
1/2 cup	unsalted butter, chilled	120 mL
1/4 cup	iced water	60 mL

The filling:

1	large egg	1
3/4 cup	sugar	180 mL
2 Tbsp.	all-purpose flour	30 mL
1 cup	sour cream or crème fraîche	240 mL
1 tsp.	vanilla	5 mL
1/4 tsp.	salt	1.2 mL
2 1/2 cups	fresh blueberries	600 mL

The topping:

6 Tbsp.	all-purpose flour	90 mL
4 Tbsp.	unsalted butter	60 mL
4 Tbsp.	sliced almonds	60 mL
2 Tbsp.	brown sugar	30 mL

To make the crust, mix the flour, sugar and salt together in a bowl. Add the butter and cut in until the mixture is mealy. Sprinkle in the water, stirring with a fork until clumps form. Gather the dough gently into a ball. Flatten and wrap in plastic wrap. Chill for 30 minutes.

On a floured surface, using a floured rolling pin, roll out the dough into a 13-inch (33-cm) circle. Transfer to a 9-inch (23-cm) pie pan. Crimp the edge and chill for 30 minutes.

Preheat the oven to 400°F (200°C). Line the crust with foil and fill with dried beans or pie weights. Bake until the sides are set, 12-15 minutes. Remove from the oven and remove the foil and weights.

To make the filling, beat the egg, sugar and flour together. Beat in the sour cream or crème fraîche, vanilla and salt. Stir in the blueberries and pour the mixture into the prepared crust. Bake on the middle shelf for 25-30 minutes, until the filling is just set.

For the topping, mix the flour and butter with your fingertips in a small bowl until small clumps form. Mix in the almonds and brown sugar. Sprinkle over the top of the pie and bake until the topping browns lightly, 12-15 minutes. Cool to room temperature before serving.

Sour Cherry Clafouti

A clafouti is a cross between a pancake and a custard. Remember, fresh sour cherries are here only for a few weeks every year, so take advantage of them! Later on in the year, you can use blueberries, plums or peaches.

Serves 6

4	large eggs	4
1/2 cup	sugar	120 mL
	pinch of salt	
1/3 cup	flour	80 mL
1 cup	milk	240 mL
4 Tbsp.	unsalted butter, melted	60 mL
1 tsp.	vanilla extract	5 mL
1 lb.	sour cherries, pitted	454 g

Preheat the oven to 325°F (165°C). Butter a 9-inch (23-cm) glass pie pan.

Beat the eggs, sugar and salt together. Add the flour and beat until smooth. Slowly whisk in the milk, butter and vanilla.

Scatter the cherries over the bottom of the pan and evenly spread the batter on top. Bake in the center of the oven for 40-50 minutes until the clafouti is just set in the center and golden brown on top. Cool before serving. Serve with vanilla ice cream if you wish.

Mango, Macadamia and Coconut Upside-Down Cake

This cake has three of my favorite things: mango, coconut and upside-down. You can use almonds or walnuts in place of the macadamia nuts.

Makes 1 10-inch (25-cm) cake

1/4 cup	unsalted butter, at room temperature	60 mL
3/4 cup	dark brown sugar, packed	180 mL
1/2 cup	unsweetened large-flake coconut	120 mL
1/2 cup	roasted macadamia nuts	120 mL
2	firm, ripe mangoes, peeled, pitted and cut into 1/2-inch (1.2-cm) cubes	2
1 3/4 cups	all-purpose flour	425 mL
1 tsp.	baking powder	5 mL
1 tsp.	baking soda	5 mL
1/4 tsp.	salt	1.2 mL
1/2 cup	unsalted butter	120 mL
1 cup	sugar	240 mL
2	large eggs	2
1 tsp.	vanilla	5 mL
1 cup	yogurt	240 mL

Preheat the oven to 375°F (190°C). Cut the unsalted butter into small pieces and place in a 10-inch (25-cm) deep cake pan. Place in the oven until the butter melts. Remove from the oven and sprinkle the brown sugar evenly over the butter. Sprinkle the coconut and macadamia nuts evenly over the brown sugar, then the mango.

Sift the flour, baking powder, baking soda and salt together. With an electric mixer, cream the butter until light. Gradually add the sugar and beat for 1 minute. Add the eggs one at a time, then the vanilla. Beat in the yogurt on low speed, then add the flour mixture in 3 batches until just combined. Scrape the batter over the topping in the pan.

Bake for 40-45 minutes, until a cake tester comes out clean. Cool on a rack for a few minutes. Run a knife around the edge of the pan and turn out onto a large plate. Serve warm or at room temperature.

Fall

A Small Feast for the First Sweater

Chicken Stew with Dumplings

Mashed Potatoes and Carrots

Butterscotch Pudding

When the air first starts to feel chilly, when the stars look crystal clear, when there is a whiff of smoke in the night air—these are all reasons for the Feast of the First Sweater. Warm, steamy, soft, smooth: all the textures required to ease us into the chilly fall season.

Chicken Stew with Dumplings

If you like a clear stew, omit the egg yolks and cream.

Serves 4

2 1/2 lbs.	bone-in chicken parts, legs or breasts or both	1.1 kg
6 cups	chicken stock	1.5 lL
1 cup	onion, coarsely chopped	240 mL
1 cup	celery, coarsely chopped	240 mL
2	cloves garlic, minced	2
1	bay leaf	1
2	small sprigs fresh thyme	2
1 tsp.	salt	5 mL
1 1/2 cups	flour	360 mL
2 tsp.	baking powder	10 mL
1/4 tsp.	salt	1.2 mL
2 Tbsp.	unsalted butter	30 mL
1 Tbsp.	fresh parsley, finely chopped	15 mL
1	egg	1
1/3 cup	milk	80 mL
2	egg yolks	2
2 Tbsp.	whipping cream	30 mL
1/4 cup	chives or green onion tops, finely chopped	60 mL
	salt and pepper to taste	

Trim the fat from the chicken pieces and remove the skin if you wish. If using whole chicken breasts, cut through the breast bone, then cut each piece in half crosswise. Cut legs through the joint into 2 pieces.

In a large pot, bring the chicken stock to a boil over high heat. Add the chicken, onion, celery, garlic, bay leaf, thyme and salt. Turn down to a simmer and cook the chicken until the juice runs clear when pierced with a fork, 30-40 minutes, keeping in mind that the breasts will cook faster than the legs. Remove the chicken pieces to a bowl as they are done. Add a bit of the cooking juice to keep them moist; cover and keep warm.

Skim the fat from the cooking liquid and strain through a sieve. Return to the pot.

To make the dumplings, combine the flour, baking powder and salt. Cut in the butter with 2 knives or a pastry blender until it looks like cornmeal. Stir in the parsley. Beat the egg and milk together well; add to the flour mixture and stir only until combined. Bring the cooking liquid to a boil. With an oiled spoon, scoop up small dumplings and push them off with another spoon into the cooking liquid. Cover and turn down to a simmer. Cook for 10 minutes, or until a toothpick inserted in a dumpling comes out clean. Remove from the pot and place to one side of deep, heated soup plates. Place the warm chicken to the other side.

Beat together the egg yolks, cream and chives or green onion. Remove the simmering liquid from the heat and quickly whisk in the yolk mixture. Adjust the seasoning and pour over the chicken. Serve immediately.

Mashed Potatoes and Carrots

My grandmother made this for me, plain and simple with a bit of butter melting in a small crater in the middle.

Serves 4-6

1 1/2 lbs.	russet potatoes, peeled and cut into 1-inch (2.5-cm) cubes	680 g
1/2 lb.	small carrots, peeled and thinly sliced	227 g
2 tsp.	salt	10 mL
4 Tbsp.	unsalted butter	60 mL
1/2 cup	hot milk	120 mL
	salt and pepper to taste	

Place the vegetables in a large pot. Cover them with cold water, add the salt and bring to a boil. Cook until the potatoes are completely tender, 15-20 minutes. Drain well and return to the pot. Mash until the potatoes are completely smooth; the carrots will remain in small pieces. Add the butter and beat until incorporated, then stir in the milk. Season to taste.

Butterscotch Pudding

Make the pudding the day before or early the same day. Serve with whipped cream if you like.

In the interest of having leftovers, this makes 8 servings

1/4 cup	water	60 mL
2 tsp.	gelatin	10 mL
5 Tbsp.	cornstarch	75 mL
2 cups	milk	475 mL
1/4 tsp.	salt	1.2 mL
1 1/4 cups	dark brown sugar, well-packed	300 mL
1 cup	whipping cream	240 mL
6 Tbsp.	unsalted butter	90 mL
3	large egg yolks	3
1 Tbsp.	pure vanilla extract	15 mL

Place the water in a small bowl. Sprinkle the gelatin over the top and set aside while you are preparing the rest of the pudding.

Whisk the cornstarch with 1/2 cup (120 mL) milk until smooth. Place the remaining milk, salt, brown sugar, whipping cream and butter in a large, heavy-bottomed pot. Bring to a simmer, stirring frequently. Whisk in the cornstarch mixture until it comes to a boil. Beat the egg yolks together and whisk a bit of the hot mixture into the egg yolks. Remove from the heat, then whisk the egg-yolk mixture into the pot. Place back on the heat and, without boiling, whisk for 30 seconds. Remove from the heat. Add the gelatin mixture and vanilla; whisk until dissolved.

Pour the pudding into 8 cups or ramekins. Cool to room temperature, cover and refrigerate up to 6 hours or overnight.

Feast for the Last Tomato and the Waning of the Light

Roast Leg of Pork with Crackling

Rutabaga Purée with Balsamic Vinegar

Braised Escarole with Parmesan Crust

Cabbage, Apple and Blue Cheese Salad

Sweet Potato Custard

*W*hen you need a super feast to ease you into winter, this is the one. It is a feast for shorter days, a feast to say good-bye to summer tomatoes. Salmon, halibut and prawn season is over, oysters start to be at their best, and root vegetables, cabbages and potatoes are ready to be roasted, braised and mashed. This is a season of gentle stews, crisp slaws, and oysters prepared in many ways.

As a guideline, marinate the pork, prepare the cabbage salad and cook and chill the sweet potato custard. Wash and chop the escarole, grate the Parmesan cheese and make the breadcrumbs. If you like roast pork with applesauce, make your own several days before, or use store-bought. Make the rutabaga purée. The escarole can be cooked with the roast and the purée heated along with it. When the pork and purée are heated, they are removed and the escarole is gratinéed. Just before serving, glaze the custard.

Roast Leg of Pork with Crackling

T here is nothing quite so beauteous as this. And the aroma! Distract yourself by catching up on the ironing.

Serves more than 8, but you can make hot pork sandwiches with the leftovers

1	small whole pork leg with skin, about 10 lbs. (4.5 kg)	1
1/4 cup	salt	60 mL
1/4 cup	fresh sage leaves, coarsely chopped	60 mL
8	cloves garlic, minced	8
2 Tbsp.	coarsely crushed black pepper	30 mL
1 Tbsp.	coarsely crushed fennel seeds	15 mL
1/2 cup	vegetable oil	120 mL
2 cups	dry white wine	475 mL

The day before serving, trim any extra fat from the leg of pork. Turn the pork with the shank end away from you and imagine the roast as a leaf with a middle rib and the smaller ribs branching away from the middle. Using a very sharp knife, score the pork on each side of the midrib, following the imaginary smaller ribs, starting at the middle and continuing down along both sides of the roast without the cuts meeting in the center. Make the cuts 1 inch (2.5 cm) apart and about 1/2 inch (1.2 cm) deep. Combine the remaining ingredients except for the wine, and rub all over the pork and into the incisions. Cover and refrigerate overnight.

Five to six hours before serving, preheat the oven to 325°F (165°C). Brush the marinade lightly off the meat and transfer the roast to a large roasting pan. Roast for 4 1/2 hours or 25 minutes per pound (454 g). After 1 hour, pour the wine into the pan and baste the roast with pan juices every 1/2 hour. Check for doneness by inserting an instant-read thermometer into the thickest part of the leg. It should read 165-170°F (74-78°C).

Remove the roast from the pan and let it rest for 10 minutes. Remove the fat with a spoon or a fat separator. Transfer the juices to a pot and keep warm over low heat. Check the flavor of the pan juices, adding water if they seem too strong. Remove the crackling and trim off and discard any fat. Cut a V-shaped notch of meat out of the roast just above the shank end, and slice through the meat, freeing the slices by making a horizontal cut under the slices, along the top of the bone. Cut the crackling into strips and arrange with the meat on a heated platter. Serve the pan juices separately.

Rutabaga Purée with Balsamic Vinegar

Rutabagas are those large golden and purple roots that are often called turnips. Turnips are smaller, white-bottomed and purple-topped.
Quarter the rutabagas with a cleaver or large heavy knife before peeling them. This makes them much easier to handle. The balsamic vinegar balances the sweetness of the vegetable.

Serves 8

4 lbs.	rutabagas, peeled and cut into 1-inch (2.5-cm) cubes	1.8 kg
6 Tbsp.	unsalted butter	90 mL
2 Tbsp.	sour cream or crème fraîche (page 205)	30 mL
	salt and pepper to taste	
2 Tbsp.	balsamic vinegar	30 mL

Place the rutabaga in a pot and cover with cold water. Cook at a moderate boil until the rutabaga is tender, 45 minutes to 1 hour. Drain well.

Purée the rutabaga in a food processor in 2 batches until completely smooth, or mash by hand. Return to the pot and stir in 1/2 the butter, the sour cream or crème fraîche and salt and pepper to taste. Stir over low heat until hot. Transfer to a large gratin or baking dish. You can make the purée up to 2 days ahead, cover and refrigerate. Bring to room temperature and reheat, covered, in a 400°F (200°C) oven for 20-30 minutes.

To finish the purée, melt the remaining butter and balsamic vinegar together over low heat. Drizzle over the purée and serve immediately.

Braised Escarole with Parmesan Crust

While escarole may seem tough as a salad vegetable, it is excellent steamed and served with lemon or braised and covered with a crunchy Parmesan crust.

Serves 8

4 Tbsp.	olive oil	60 mL
1 cup	onion, thinly sliced	240 mL
2	large heads escarole, washed, dried and cut into 2-inch (5-cm) pieces	2
4	cloves garlic, minced	4
1 Tbsp.	fresh rosemary, chopped	15 mL
1 tsp.	grated lemon zest	5 mL
1/2 cup	dry white wine	120 mL
1 1/2 cups	chicken stock	360 mL
	salt and pepper to taste	
1/2 cup	fresh breadcrumbs	120 mL
1/2 cup	freshly grated Parmesan cheese	120 mL

Preheat the oven to 325°F (165°C). In a large frying pan, heat the olive oil over medium heat. Add the onion and sauté until lightly browned. Add the escarole and garlic and cook until the escarole wilts. Add the rosemary, lemon zest, white wine and chicken stock.

Bring to a boil, season lightly with salt and pepper and transfer to a wide, shallow baking dish. Cover and place in the oven. Bake for 40-50 minutes, until most of the liquid is absorbed. Remove the dish from the oven and increase the temperature to 400°F (200°C). Combine the breadcrumbs and Parmesan cheese and sprinkle evenly over the top of the escarole. Bake until the top is golden brown and crisp, about 15 minutes.

Cabbage, Apple and Blue Cheese Salad

This is a condiment-style salad that goes very well with pork roast.

Serves 8

2 lbs.	red cabbage, cored and finely shredded	900 g
1/2 cup	cider vinegar	120 mL
1 tsp.	salt	5 mL
10 cups	boiling water	2.4 L
6 Tbsp.	cider vinegar	90 mL
2 Tbsp.	Dijon mustard	30 mL
2 tsp.	sugar	10 mL
	salt and pepper to taste	
1/2 cup	vegetable oil	120 mL
2	large apples, peeled, cut in half, cored and thinly sliced	2
1/2 cup	red onion, finely chopped	120 mL
1/2 cup	blue cheese, crumbled	120 mL

In a large bowl, combine the cabbage, 1/2 cup (120 mL) vinegar and salt. Toss until well combined and let sit for 5 minutes. Pour the boiling water over the cabbage, let sit for 3 minutes, drain well and pat dry.

Whisk the 6 Tbsp. (90 mL) vinegar, Dijon mustard and sugar together. Season with salt and pepper. Slowly whisk in the oil. Add the dressing along with the apples and onion to the cabbage and toss well. Cover and refrigerate until ready to serve or overnight.

When ready to serve, transfer to a serving bowl and sprinkle with the blue cheese.

Sweet Potato Custard

This is a cross between a pumpkin pie and a sweet potato crème brûlée.

Serves 8

1/4 cup	light brown sugar, packed	60 mL
1	sweet potato, about 1/2 lb. (227 g)	1
9	large egg yolks	9
1/2 cup	sugar	120 mL
1/2 tsp.	cinnamon	2.5 mL
1/4 tsp.	ground nutmeg	1.2 mL
1/4 tsp.	salt	1.2 mL
1/2 cup	half-and-half cream	120 mL
2 1/2 cups	heavy cream	600 mL
2 tsp.	pure vanilla extract	10 mL

One day or up to one week before, spread the brown sugar out onto a plate and let it dry overnight. Grind the brown sugar in a food processor or spice grinder until fine. Cover tightly and keep at room temperature.

Preheat the oven to 400°F (200°C). Prick the sweet potato with a fork and bake for 1 hour, until completely tender. Remove from the oven and cool. Peel the potato and purée in a food processor or mash by hand until completely smooth. Turn the oven down to 300°F (150°C).

Whisk the egg yolks, sugar, cinnamon, nutmeg and salt together by hand or with an electric mixer until pale and thick, 4-5 minutes. Whisk in the sweet potato purée until smooth, then the creams and vanilla. Strain through a sieve into a round, 10-inch (25-cm) glass or ceramic quiche or gratin dish. Place in a larger pan and add boiling water to come halfway up the side of the baking dish. Bake for 35-40 minutes, until the custard is just set and barely jiggly in the middle. Remove from the oven and the water bath. Cool completely. Cover and refrigerate for at least 4 hours or overnight.

Preheat the broiler. Sprinkle the prepared brown sugar evenly over the top of the custard. Broil for about 1 minute, until the sugar is lightly caramelized. Serve immediately.

Thanksgiving Feast

Roast Turkey with Pancetta, Rosemary
and Garlic

Potato and Celery Root Gratin

Lentil Stew with Spinach

Grape Focaccia

Steamed Pumpkin Pudding with
Cool Maple Sauce

Thanksgiving has always been my favorite traditional feast day because it is free of pressure. It is the day to get together with friends and family; to cook a Grand Leisurely Feast. If you have forgotten to order the turkey, switch gears and serve the Christmas Feast instead. The dishes from the Feast for the Last Tomato, Thanksgiving Feast and Christmas Feast can be exchanged for one another or mixed and matched to suit your preferences or mood. If you have the inclination, prepare two desserts. Baked Apples with Mascarpone and Amaretti, page 195, would nicely complement the Steamed Pumpkin Pudding and is easy to prepare.

Freshly shucked oysters on the half shell with lemon and freshly grated horseradish would be the ideal starter to this feast, if you feel you need one.

Roast Turkey with Pancetta, Rosemary and Garlic

This is one of my favorite methods of roasting turkey. It emerges from the oven well seasoned and succulent.

Serves 8

1	15-lb. (7-kg) turkey	1
1/2 lb.	pancetta	227 g
1/2 cup	fresh rosemary leaves	120 mL
4	whole heads garlic	4
6	cloves garlic, minced	6
1/2 tsp.	salt	2.5 mL
1 tsp.	coarsely ground black pepper	5 mL
	olive oil	
2 cups	dry red wine	475 mL
1/2 cup	shallots, finely chopped	120 mL

Preheat the oven to 350°F (175°C).

Rinse the turkey and pat dry. Finely chop half the pancetta and cut the other half into large chunks. Stuff the large chunks of pancetta, half the rosemary leaves and the whole heads of garlic into the cavity of the turkey.

Transfer the finely chopped pancetta to the workbowl of a food processor with the remaining rosemary, minced garlic, salt and pepper. Pulse until everything is finely chopped.

Loosen the skin of the turkey over the breast and around the legs. Slide the pancetta mixture over the breast and legs, under the skin, patting it out evenly. Transfer to a roasting pan and rub the turkey with olive oil. Tie the legs loosely.

Roast for 3-3 1/2 hours (see How Do I Know When It's Done?), basting the turkey with 1/2 cup (120 mL) of the red wine every 30 minutes. After the second basting, scatter the shallots in the bottom of the roasting pan.

Remove the turkey from the roasting pan. Degrease the juices with a fat separator or skim with a spoon. Strain through a sieve into a pot; keep warm over low heat and adjust the seasoning.

Remove the whole garlic from the cavity and separate the cloves. Remove and discard the pancetta and rosemary, or save to use in soup. Carve the turkey into slices and garnish with the cloves of garlic, which are meant to be eaten. Serve with the pan juices on the side.

How Do I Know When It's Done?

One of the questions I'm asked frequently is, "How do I know when it's done?" My answer is to buy yourself an instant-read thermometer and use the recommendations below for meats and fish. Having an instant-read thermometer takes all the anxiety and guesswork out of cooking meat.

To use it, insert the thermometer into the thickest part of the meat so the point is in the middle, and give it a few seconds to adjust.

105°F–110°F (40°C–43°C) **Rare.**
115°F–125°F (46°C–52°C) **Medium-rare.** I prefer 115°F.
130°F–140°F (54°C–60°C) **Medium.**
Over 150°F (65°C) **Well done!**

Roasts, big steaks and large birds should sit for at least 10-15 minutes before slicing. As the meat rests, it continues to cook, so keep this in mind when checking the temperature. It is recommended that poultry be cooked to 180°F (82°C). I personally find chicken and turkey cooked to this temperature to be overcooked and extremely dry, but I can't tell you to do as I do in this instance.

Potato and Celery Root Gratin

Celeriac are knobbly, hairy root vegetables that appear for sale in the fall. They have a distinct celery flavor and are delicious mixed with potatoes as a purée or in a gratin. The traditional French celeriac remoulade is made from julienned celeriac, tossed with a mustardy vinaigrette.

Serves 8

1 1/2 lbs.	celery root, washed	680 g
1 1/2 lbs.	russet potatoes	680 g
3/4 cup	whipping cream	180 mL
1 Tbsp.	Dijon mustard	15 mL
1 tsp.	salt	5 mL
	pepper to taste	
1	clove garlic, minced	1
1/4 tsp.	nutmeg	1.2 mL
1 cup	grated Swiss or Gruyère cheese	240 mL

Preheat the oven to 375°F (190°C). Butter a 2-qt. (2-L) gratin dish.

Peel the celery root, cut in quarters and remove the core if spongy. Thinly slice crosswise. Bring a large pot of water to a boil and add the celery root. Cook until barely tender, about 5 minutes. Remove with a slotted spoon to a colander to drain. Keep the water boiling.

Peel the potatoes, cut into 1/4-inch (.6-cm) slices and transfer to the boiling water. Cook until they are barely tender, about 5 minutes. Transfer with a slotted spoon to the same colander. Reserve 1 1/4 cups (300 mL) of the cooking liquid.

Gently toss the celeriac and potatoes together. Spread out evenly in the baking dish. Bring the reserved cooking water, cream, mustard, salt, pepper, garlic and nutmeg to a simmer and pour over the vegetables. Bake until the sauce is bubbly and the vegetables tender, about 45 minutes. Sprinkle with the grated cheese and bake for 15 minutes longer.

Lentil Stew with Spinach

*L*ook for the small, brown "French" lentils called Le Puy, *which are, for the most part, grown in Saskatchewan. They cook quickly and retain their shape.*

Serves 8

2 Tbsp.	olive oil	30 mL
4	cloves garlic, minced	4
6 cups	unsalted chicken stock	1.5 L
2 cups	small brown lentils, picked over for stones and rinsed	480 mL
1	small onion, peeled and stuck with 2 whole cloves	1
	salt and pepper to taste	
2 Tbsp.	olive oil	30 mL
2 cups	onion, thinly sliced into half-moons	475 mL
1 lb.	fresh spinach, stems removed, coarsely chopped	454 g
	pinch of cayenne pepper	
1/2	small lemon, thinly sliced into rounds, seeds removed	1/2

In a large heavy pot, heat 2 Tbsp. (30 mL) olive oil over medium heat. Add the garlic and stir until it just starts to turn golden. Add the chicken stock, lentils and the onion with 2 cloves. Bring to a boil and skim off any foam that rises to the top. Simmer over low heat, partially covered, until the lentils are tender, 30-40 minutes. Stir occasionally and add more liquid if necessary to keep the lentils moist. Discard the onion and season with salt and pepper. The stew may be prepared up to this point several days in advance. Cool, cover and refrigerate. Heat to a simmer before proceeding.

While the lentils are cooking, heat 2 Tbsp. (30 mL) olive oil in a heavy, preferably nonstick pan over medium heat. Add the sliced onion and sauté until it is a deep brown. Drain through a sieve and reserve.

Add the spinach to the lentils. Cover and simmer until the spinach wilts. Stir in the cayenne, lemon slices and browned onion.

Grape Focaccia

This is a delicious accompaniment to the turkey; you may want to make two of them. I like to serve a cheese course with Grand Feasts—the grape focaccia is an ideal foil. I generally choose cheeses that are ripe and ready and arrange them on large edible leaves on a platter a few hours before dinner. This allows them to warm up and ensures that they are eaten at their best flavor.

Makes 1 10- by 15-inch (25- by 38-cm) bread

1/3 cup	olive oil	80 mL
2 Tbsp.	fresh rosemary leaves, coarsely chopped	30 mL
2 1/2 tsp.	dry, regular yeast	12.5 mL
1 cup	lukewarm water	240 mL
1/4 cup	sugar	60 mL
1 tsp.	salt	5 mL
3 cups	unbleached white flour	720 mL
	cornmeal for dusting the pan	
2 cups	seedless Red Flame grapes	475 mL
1 cup	walnut pieces	240 mL

In a small frying pan, heat the oil over medium heat until hot, 2-3 minutes. Add the rosemary and remove from the heat. Cool completely, then strain the oil. Discard the rosemary leaves.

In a large bowl, sprinkle the yeast over the water. Let stand for 10 minutes. Stir in the rosemary oil, sugar and salt. Beat in the flour, a cup at a time. Turn the dough out onto a lightly floured surface and knead until smooth and elastic, adding as little flour as possible, about 8-10 minutes. Transfer the dough to a lightly oiled bowl; turn to coat with the oil. Cover with a towel and let rise in a warm place until doubled in bulk, about 45 minutes.

Preheat the oven to 375°F (190°C). Lightly oil a 10- by 15-inch (25- by 38-cm) jelly-roll pan and sprinkle lightly with cornmeal. Punch down the dough and transfer it to the prepared pan. Pat, press and stretch the dough out to fit the pan. Let it relax every minute or so, then continue; this will make it easier to stretch. Scatter the grapes and walnuts over the surface and press lightly into the dough. Cover with a towel and let rise for 30 minutes.

Bake for 30-35 minutes, until lightly browned and crisp. Remove from the pan and transfer the focaccia to a rack to cool.

Steamed Pumpkin Pudding with Cool Maple Sauce

The pudding may be made in advance and frozen. Thaw completely and resteam in the mold for 20 minutes to heat through.

Serves 8

2 1/4 cups	flour	535 mL
1 3/4 tsp.	baking powder	9 mL
1 1/2 tsp.	cinnamon	7.5 mL
1 tsp.	ground dried ginger	5 mL
1/2 tsp.	ground nutmeg	2.5 mL
1/4 tsp.	ground cloves	1.2 mL
1/2 tsp.	salt	2.5 mL
3/4 cup	unsalted butter at room temperature	180 mL
2 cups	light brown sugar, packed	475 mL
3	large eggs	3
1 1/2 cups	canned pumpkin purée	360 mL
1 cup	pecans, coarsely chopped	240 mL
1 recipe	Cool Maple Sauce (page 124)	1 recipe

Generously butter a 2 1/2-qt (2.5-l) pudding mold and lid. Prepare a large, lidded pot with boiling water and a trivet in the bottom.

With a whisk, stir the flour, baking powder, cinnamon, ginger, nutmeg, cloves and salt together.

In a large bowl, beat the butter until smooth with an electric mixer. Add the brown sugar and beat until light. Beat in the eggs one at a time. Beat in the pumpkin purée until thoroughly blended. On low speed, add the dry ingredients and mix until just blended. Stir in the pecans.

Transfer to the prepared mold and smooth the top. Clip on the lid and place in the pot. The water should come halfway up the side of the mold. Cover with a lid and steam on medium heat, adding more boiling water if necessary, until a tester comes out clean, about 2 hours. Transfer the mold to a rack and cool for 10 minutes. Loosen the pudding with a small knife and turn out onto the rack. Serve with Cool Maple Sauce on the side.

Cool Maple Sauce

*Also delicious
over ice cream or
on toast.*

Makes 3 cups (720 mL)

8	large egg yolks	8
1/2 cup	pure maple syrup	120 mL
	pinch of salt	
1 cup	half-and-half cream	240 mL
1 cup	whipping cream	240 mL
1 tsp.	pure vanilla extract	5 mL
2 Tbsp.	walnut liqueur	30 mL

In a large bowl that will fit over a pot of simmering water but not touch the water, whisk the egg yolks, maple syrup and salt together until well blended. Place over the pot of simmering water and cook, whisking constantly, until the yolks thicken and increase in volume, about 8 minutes. While you are whisking, heat the creams to a simmer in a heavy pot. Whisk the hot cream into the yolk mixture and continue to whisk for 2 more minutes. Remove from the heat and add the vanilla and walnut liqueur. Cool, cover and refrigerate until ready to serve. The sauce may be prepared a day in advance.

Salmon Stew

Serve over Corn Pancakes, page 93, or with Buttermilk Biscuits, page 207.

Serves 4

5 Tbsp.	unsalted butter	75 ml
2	leeks, white and light green part only, thinly sliced (see A Bit About Leeks, page 191)	2
1 cup	zucchini, cut into 1/4-inch (.6-cm) dice	240 ml
1/4 cup	celery, finely diced	60 ml
1/4 cup	carrots, finely diced	60 ml
1/2 lb.	cultivated mushrooms, thinly sliced	227 g
3 Tbsp.	all-purpose flour	45 ml
2 cups	canned or bottled clam nectar	475 ml
1 1/2 lbs.	boneless, skinless salmon filets, cut into 1/2-inch (1.2-cm) cubes	680 g
1/2 cup	whipping cream, crème fraîche (page 205), half-and-half cream or milk	120 ml
	salt and pepper to taste	
2	green onions, thinly sliced	2
1 Tbsp.	fresh parsley, finely chopped	15 ml
2 Tbsp.	fresh dill, finely chopped	30 ml

In a large pot, melt 3 Tbsp. (45 ml) of the butter over medium heat. Add the leeks, zucchini, celery and carrots. Cook until the leeks are soft but not brown.

In a separate frying pan, melt the remaining butter over high heat; add the mushrooms and sauté until the mushrooms are tender and any liquid they have thrown off has evaporated. Reserve.

Add the flour to the leeks and stir for a minute. Turn the heat to high and slowly whisk in the clam nectar. Bring to a boil, turn down the heat and simmer for 10 minutes, stirring occasionally. Add the salmon and mushrooms; simmer until the salmon is cooked through, about 10 minutes, stirring occasionally. Add the cream, crème fraîche or milk and season with salt and pepper. When the stew is piping hot, add the green onion, parsley and dill. Serve in heated bowls.

Halibut with Pine Nut and Parmesan Crust

Make this before halibut season ends, usually in October.

Serves 4

1/2 cup	pine nuts, coarsely chopped	120 mL
4 Tbsp.	freshly grated Parmesan cheese	60 mL
1 Tbsp.	fresh basil, finely chopped	15 mL
1	clove garlic, minced	1
1 Tbsp.	olive oil	15 mL
4	6-oz. (170-g) halibut filets	4
	salt to taste	

Preheat the oven to 425°F (220°C). Combine the pine nuts, Parmesan cheese, basil, garlic and olive oil. Place the halibut filets on a baking sheet and season with salt. Pat the pine nut mixture onto the halibut, pressing lightly to make it adhere. Bake in the middle of the oven for 10-15 minutes, until the fish is opaque all the way through.

Clams Steamed in Spicy Coconut Lime Broth

This is also very good with mussels and can be served with steamed rice for a main course. It is quickly assembled and cooked—bonus!

Serves 4

1	14-oz. (398-mL) can unsweetened coconut milk	1
1/2 cup	canned or bottled clam nectar	120 mL
1 cup	canned plum tomatoes, well drained and finely diced	240 mL
1 Tbsp.	fresh cilantro leaves	15 mL
2	green onions, thinly sliced	2
1 Tbsp.	fresh ginger, grated	15 mL
1/2 tsp.	turmeric	2.5 mL
1	jalapeño pepper, finely chopped	1
2 Tbsp.	freshly squeezed lime juice	30 mL
1	lime, thinly sliced	1
3 lbs.	fresh Manila clams, scrubbed	1.4 kg

In a large pot combine all the ingredients except the clams. Bring to a boil and add the clams. Cover and cook until the clams open, shaking the pot occasionally. Ladle the clams and broth into heated bowls and serve.

Prawns Smothered in Charred Sweet Red Pepper and Tomato Sauce

Charring the peppers and tomatoes gives a buttery smooth texture to the final sauce. Leaving the skins on lends a slightly sharp edge that combines beautifully with the sweet prawns. The ultimate resting place for these prawns is on a bed of creamy polenta but pasta, rice or mashed potatoes would make a very agreeable bed as well.

Serves 4

1 lb.	ripe plum tomatoes	454 g
2	large sweet red peppers	2
2	anchovies	2
1	dried crushed red chili (or to taste)	1
3 Tbsp.	olive oil	45 mL
1/2 cup	onion, finely chopped	120 mL
3	cloves garlic, minced	3
	salt to taste	
1 lb.	large prawns, peeled	454 g
12	fresh basil leaves	12

Preheat the broiler and adjust the oven rack to approximately 6 inches (15 cm) below the heat source. Place the tomatoes and peppers on a baking sheet and broil them, turning to blacken the skins on all sides. Remove from the broiler and cool.

Keeping the blackened skins on the peppers and tomatoes, cut them in half and remove the seeds. Place in a sieve to drain for 1/2 hour. Transfer the peppers and tomatoes to a food processor or blender along with the anchovies and chili pepper and purée until smooth. The mixture will be quite thick.

In a medium-sized pot, heat the olive oil over medium heat. Add the onion and garlic and sauté until the onion is translucent. Add the tomato and pepper mixture and simmer over low heat for 1/2 hour. Taste and season with salt. This mixture may be prepared up to a day in advance.

When you are ready to finish the dish, bring the tomato and pepper sauce to a boil. Add the prawns and stir until they become opaque, 2-3 minutes. Stir in the basil leaves and serve immediately.

Risotto with Prawns, Dungeness Crab and Marinated Scallops

The marinated scallops make your tastebuds come to attention—like eating pickled ginger between bites of sushi.

Serves 4

1/2 lb.	large scallops, foot removed, sliced in half crosswise	227 g
4 Tbsp.	freshly squeezed lemon juice	60 mL
1/8 tsp.	salt	.5 mL
1/2 tsp.	fresh tarragon, finely chopped	2.5 mL
6 cups	chicken stock	1.5 L
3 Tbsp.	butter	45 mL
1 Tbsp.	vegetable oil	15 mL
2 Tbsp.	onion, finely chopped	30 mL
1 1/2 cups	arborio rice	360 mL
	salt to taste	
1 lb.	large prawns, peeled and deveined if necessary	454 g
1/2 lb.	Dungeness crab meat	227 g
1/4 cup	freshly grated Parmesan cheese	60 mL

Place the scallops in a bowl. Add the lemon juice and salt. Mix well, cover and refrigerate for up to 4 hours. Before making the risotto, drain the scallops well and mix with the tarragon.

Bring the chicken stock to a simmer. In a large heavy pot, melt 2 Tbsp. (30 mL) of the butter and the oil over medium heat. Add the onion and sauté until translucent but not browned. Add the rice and stir until it is well coated with the butter. Add 1/2 cup (120 mL) of the hot stock and stir until the stock is absorbed and the rice is creamy. Continue stirring, adding the stock by half-cups until the rice is creamy yet firm to the bite. You may not need all the stock. Season with salt. Add the prawns and stir until they are opaque, 2-3 minutes. Stir in the Dungeness crab, Parmesan cheese and the remaining butter. Transfer to heated bowls and top with the marinated scallops. Serve immediately.

Grilled Turkey Salad with Basil Dressing

A great whole meal salad. You can use chicken breasts or pork tenderloin in place of the turkey.

Serves 6-8

4	medium shallots, peeled and thinly sliced	4
2 Tbsp.	Dijon mustard	30 mL
3 Tbsp.	cider vinegar	45 mL
2 tsp.	honey	10 mL
1/2 tsp.	salt	2.5 mL
1 cup	vegetable oil	240 mL
1/4 cup	fresh basil leaves	60 mL
1/2	small boneless, skinless turkey breast, about 1 1/2 lbs. (680 g)	1/2
	salt and pepper to taste	
2	sweet yellow peppers, cored and cut into 1-inch (2.5-cm) strips	2
2	medium, ripe tomatoes, cored and cut into 8 wedges each	2
1 lb.	new potatoes, cooked, cooled and cut into quarters	454 g
1/2	English cucumber, cut into 1/4-inch (.6-cm) slices	1/2
1 lb.	baby beets, cooked, peeled and cut into quarters	454 g

To make the dressing, combine the shallots, mustard, vinegar, honey and salt in the work bowl of a food processor or blender. With the motor on, add the vegetable oil in a slow steady stream. When all the oil has been incorporated, add the basil and pulse until finely chopped.

Cut the turkey breast into 1-inch (2.5-cm) slices against the grain. Brush lightly with vegetable oil and season with salt and pepper. Preheat the barbecue or broiler. Grill or broil the turkey slices until done, about 3-5 minutes on each side. While the turkey is cooking, grill or broil the yellow peppers until a few brown spots appear and the peppers are slightly softened.

Arrange all the vegetables attractively on a large platter. Cut the turkey crosswise into 1/2-inch (1.2-cm) pieces and arrange them on top of the salad. Pass the dressing separately.

Chili Chicken and Corn Stew

Serve the stew with hot Buttermilk Biscuits, page 207, and a salad. Cilantro or fresh basil can be substituted for the parsley.

Serves 4-6

1 Tbsp.	vegetable oil	15 mL
2 lbs.	boneless, skinless chicken breasts	900 g
	salt and pepper to taste	
1 Tbsp.	unsalted butter	15 mL
3 Tbsp.	all-purpose flour	45 mL
1/2 cup	onion, finely chopped	120 mL
1/4 cup	sweet red pepper, finely chopped	60 mL
1/4 cup	celery, finely chopped	60 mL
1 1/2 cups	chicken stock	360 mL
1 tsp.	chili powder	5 mL
4	fresh or canned plum tomatoes, finely chopped	4
1 cup	fresh (about 2 ears) or frozen corn kernels	240 mL
2	green onions, thinly sliced	2
1 Tbsp.	fresh parsley, chopped	15 mL

In a large frying pan, heat the oil over medium-high heat. Season the chicken breasts with salt and pepper and brown on both sides. Transfer the chicken to a plate.

Melt the butter in the pan and stir in the flour. Turn the heat to medium-low and cook the mixture until it is the color of peanut butter. Add the onion, pepper and celery and cook until the vegetables soften, 4-5 minutes. Whisk in the chicken stock and chili powder. Add the tomatoes and chicken with any juices and simmer, covered, until the chicken is cooked, 10-15 minutes. Remove the chicken from the pan and stir in the corn.

When the chicken is cool enough to handle, cut it into bite-sized pieces and return to the pan. Stir in the green onion and parsley just before serving.

Flat Roasted Duck with Charcuterie Seasonings

Serve with the Rutabaga Purée with Balsamic Vinegar, page 113, and Mashed Potatoes and Leeks with Parmesan and Romano Cheese, page 191.

Serves 4 people, 2 who like legs and 2 who like breasts, or 2 people who really like duck

1	large duck, 5-6 lbs. (2.3-2.7 kg)	1
1 Tbsp.	whole coriander seeds	15 mL
10	whole allspice berries	10
2 tsp.	whole black peppercorns	10 mL
6	whole cloves	6
1/4	whole nutmeg	1/4
2 tsp.	salt	10 mL
6	medium cloves garlic, very thinly sliced	6

Split the duck down the backbone and open it up like a book. Place breast side up and press down on the breast with the heel of your hand to flatten it out further. Remove the wings.

Combine all the spices in a mortar and pestle or spice grinder. Coarsely crush the seeds; do not grind them finely. Place the crushed seeds in a bowl and stir in the salt. Sprinkle half the spices and garlic evenly on the underside of the duck and place in a noncorrodible dish. Sprinkle the remaining spices and garlic evenly on the skin side. Cover and refrigerate overnight.

Preheat the oven to 300°F (150°C). Wipe the spices and garlic from the duck and place on a rack in a roasting pan. Roast for 1 hour. Remove from the oven and prick the skin thoroughly with a large needle. Return to the oven and roast for 1 1/2 hours longer. Remove the duck from the rack and discard the fat from the pan. Let the duck cool. It may sit for an hour at room temperature. Cut the legs from the duck and cut the breast in half lengthwise. Remove the rib cage from the breast. Preheat the broiler and position the rack 8 inches (20 cm) away from the heat. Broil until the skin is crisp, about 5 minutes. Serve immediately on heated plates.

Shepherd's Pie

This is a very grand Shepherd's Pie. It started with just a layer of creamed corn and mashed potatoes on top, then grew to mashed white and sweet potatoes, then turned into bacon and buttermilk mashed potatoes. Oh, bliss! There are a lot of steps but they can be completed over a day or even three. It makes a big pie too; think of those fabulous leftovers. You can use ground lamb instead of beef.

Serves 8

For the ground beef layer:

1 Tbsp.	unsalted butter	15 mL
1 cup	onion, finely diced	240 mL
1/2 cup	celery, finely diced	120 mL
1/2 cup	carrot, finely diced	120 mL
2	cloves garlic	2
2 lbs.	lean ground beef	900 g
1 tsp.	salt	5 mL
1/4 tsp.	freshly ground black pepper	1.2 mL
2 Tbsp.	flour	30 mL
1 cup	water or stock	240 mL

For the creamed corn layer:

2 Tbsp.	unsalted butter	30 mL
3 Tbsp.	flour	45 mL
2 1/2 cups	milk	600 mL
2 1/2 cups	fresh or frozen corn, thawed and drained	600 mL
1/2 tsp.	salt	2.5 mL

For the mashed potato layer:

3 lbs.	russet potatoes peeled and cut into chunks	1.4 kg
4 oz.	bacon, diced	113 g
4 Tbsp.	unsalted butter	60 mL
1 cup	buttermilk	240 mL
2	green onions, thinly sliced	2
	salt and pepper to taste	

To make the beef layer, melt the butter in a large pot over medium heat. Add the onion, celery, carrot and garlic and sauté until lightly browned. Add the ground beef and turn the heat to high. Cook, crumbling the beef with the back of a spoon, until it loses its raw color. Add the salt and pepper. Place the flour in a small bowl and slowly stir in the water or stock to form a lump-free mixture. Remove the beef from the heat and slowly stir in the flour mixture. Return to the heat and bring to a boil. Turn down to a simmer and cook for 20 minutes. Spread the beef mixture evenly into a 9- by 13-inch (23- by 33-cm) baking dish.

For the creamed corn layer, melt the butter in a large nonstick pot over medium heat. Stir in the flour with a whisk and cook for a few moments. Raise the heat to high and slowly dribble in the milk, whisking constantly until the mixture thickens and comes to a boil. Add the corn and salt and bring to a boil. Turn down to a simmer and cook for about 20 minutes, stirring frequently to prevent sticking. The mixture should thicken to a pancake batter consistency and become distinctly corny tasting. It may take a bit longer if you are using fresh corn. Add the salt. Spread the creamed corn over the beef mixture.

For the mashed potatoes, place the potato chunks in a large pot and cover with cold water. Salt liberally and bring to a boil. Cook until the potatoes are very tender when pierced with a fork, about 15-20 minutes. While the potatoes are cooking, cook the bacon in a small frying pan over medium-low heat until it is crisp and browned. Drain off the fat through a strainer and place the bacon on absorbent paper. Crumble when cool. Drain the potatoes and return to the pot. Mash the potatoes until smooth. Add the butter and stir until the butter is incorporated. Stir in the buttermilk, bacon and green onion and beat until smooth. Add salt and pepper. Spread the mashed potatoes over the creamed corn.

Preheat the oven to 350°F (175°C). Place the pie on the middle rack of the oven and bake for 45 minutes to 1 hour, until bubbly. Let sit for 15 minutes before serving.

Fettuccine with Sausage, Porcini Mushrooms and Green Olives

This sauce is great served over penne, rigatoni and fusilli as well.

Serves 4

1 oz.	dried porcini mushrooms	28 g
1/2 cup	boiling water	120 mL
1 Tbsp.	olive oil	15 mL
1/2 lb.	sweet Italian sausage, thinly sliced	227 g
4 Tbsp.	unsalted butter	60 mL
1	clove garlic, minced	1
1/4 lb.	cultivated mushrooms, thinly sliced	113 g
1/2 cup	chicken stock	120 mL
1 Tbsp.	fresh parsley, finely chopped	15 mL
1/2 cup	large green olives, pitted and thinly sliced	120 mL
1 lb.	dried fettuccine	454 g
	salt and pepper to taste	

Place the porcini mushrooms in a small bowl and cover with the boiling water. Let the mushrooms soak for half an hour. Remove the porcini mushrooms from the liquid and check for dirt. Coarsely chop. Strain the soaking liquid through a coffee filter to remove any sand and reserve.

Heat the olive oil in a large frying pan over high heat. Add the sausage and cook, stirring frequently, over medium heat until the sausage is browned. Remove the sausage from the pan and add the butter. When it sizzles, add the garlic, cultivated and porcini mushrooms and sauté until the mushrooms throw off their liquid, about 5 minutes. Add the sausage, the reserved porcini soaking water and the chicken stock. Bring to a boil and cook until the liquid thickens slightly, 3-5 minutes. Add the parsley and olives and remove from the heat.

Bring a large pot of water to a boil and salt liberally. It should taste like seawater. Add the fettuccine and cook, stirring occasionally, until the pasta is tender but still firm to the bite, 8-10 minutes. Drain the pasta and return to the pot. Add the sauce and stir over low heat to coat the pasta with the sauce. Transfer to heated bowls and serve.

Bow Ties with Spicy Sausage and Smoked Mozzarella

You can use a full-fat plain mozzarella or fontina cheese in place of the smoked mozzarella.

Serves 4

1 lb.	hot Italian sausage	454 g
1 Tbsp.	olive oil	15 mL
1	medium onion, thinly sliced	1
2	cloves garlic, minced	2
1 Tbsp.	tomato paste	15 mL
1/4 cup	dry white wine	60 mL
2 cups	chicken stock	475 mL
	salt and pepper to taste	
1 lb.	dried bow-tie pasta	454 g
1/2 lb.	smoked mozzarella, cut into small cubes	227 g
1 Tbsp.	fresh parsley, finely chopped	15 mL

Bring a large pot of water to a boil. Meanwhile, prepare the sauce. Remove the casings from the sausages and crumble into small pieces. In a large pot, heat the olive oil over medium heat. Add the onion and garlic and sauté until the onion is soft. Add the sausage and cook until it is lightly browned on the outside. Dissolve the tomato paste in the white wine and add to the sausage mixture. Turn the heat to high and boil for a minute. Add the chicken stock and boil until the mixture is reduced by half. Season with salt and pepper. Remove from the heat.

Add the bow ties to the boiling water and salt liberally. It should taste like seawater. Cook, stirring occasionally, until the pasta is tender but still firm to the bite, 8-10 minutes. Drain the pasta and return to the pot. Add the sauce and stir over low heat to coat the pasta with the sauce. Stir in the smoked mozzarella and parsley. Transfer to heated bowls and serve.

Pickled Potato Salad with Horseradish and Dill

A tangy salad, great with roast beef or cold cuts.

Serves 4

1 lb.	small red potatoes, thickly sliced	454 g
1/2 cup	carrots, thinly sliced	120 mL
2 Tbsp.	mayonnaise	30 mL
2 Tbsp.	yogurt	30 mL
1 tsp.	Dijon mustard	5 mL
1 tsp.	cider vinegar	5 mL
1 Tbsp.	freshly grated or prepared horseradish	15 mL
2 Tbsp.	kosher-style dill pickle, finely chopped	30 mL
1 Tbsp.	fresh dill, finely chopped	15 mL
2 Tbsp.	red onion, finely chopped	30 mL

Place the potatoes and carrots in a pot and cover them with cold salted water by a few inches (8 cm). Bring to a boil and cook until the potatoes are tender, 10-15 minutes. Drain and cool. In a large bowl, combine the mayonnaise, yogurt, mustard, vinegar, horseradish, pickle, dill and onion. Add the potatoes and carrots and toss well. Serve immediately or chill for up to 1 day.

"Tired" Tomato Salad

The tomatoes look "tired" as a result of being salted, not because they are old! Salting draws out water to leave a true tomato flavor. A great accompaniment to grilled or roasted chicken.

Serves 4

1 lb.	ripe, summer tomatoes, about 4	454 g
1 1/2 tsp.	salt	7.5 mL
3 Tbsp.	red wine vinegar	45 mL
4 Tbsp.	olive oil	60 mL
1 Tbsp.	fresh parsley, coarsely chopped	15 mL
	freshly ground black pepper to taste	

Core the tomatoes and cut them into 8 wedges each. Place the tomato wedges in a bowl and add the salt, vinegar and 2 Tbsp. (30 mL) of the olive oil. Mix gently and allow to stand for 2-4 hours.

Just before serving, drain the tomatoes in a colander and discard the juice. Mix with the remaining olive oil, parsley and pepper.

Pear Salad with Basil and Romano Cheese

A delicious combination of flavors! The pears would sit nicely beside pork or chicken and could even be served as an unusual dessert. Parmesan or asiago cheese may be substituted.

Serves 4

3	ripe pears (Bartletts are a good choice)	3
2 Tbsp.	balsamic vinegar	30 mL
1 tsp.	honey	5 mL
3 Tbsp.	olive oil	45 mL
1/4 tsp.	coarsely ground black pepper	1.2 mL
1/2 cup	Romano shavings, loosely packed	120 mL
1/4 cup	fresh basil leaves, torn into small pieces	60 mL

Peel and core the pears. Cut each into 8 wedges. Mix the balsamic vinegar with the honey, add the pears and toss to coat them with the mixture. Arrange the pears on a serving platter and drizzle with the olive oil. Scatter with the black pepper, the cheese shavings and the basil. *Note:* Make cheese shavings by drawing a vegetable peeler across a wedge of cheese.

Melon Salad with Feta, Mint and Pine Nuts

Try a full-flavored goat or sheep milk feta with this salad and use any combination of melon that is fragrant, fresh and sweet. It is divine with smoked salmon, trout or prosciutto.

Serves 6-8

1	small cantaloupe	1
1/2	honeydew melon	1/2
1 Tbsp.	lime juice	15 mL
1	small red onion, sliced into thin rings	1
1/2 cup	crumbled feta	120 mL
1/4 cup	fresh mint leaves, coarsely chopped	60 mL
1/4 cup	black olives	60 mL
2 Tbsp.	toasted pine nuts	30 mL

Peel the melons, cut in half and scoop out the seeds. Cut into 1-inch thick (2.5-cm) wedges. Cut the wedges into 1-inch (2.5-cm) triangular pieces. Place in a bowl and toss with the lime juice. Transfer to a platter. Scatter the onion rings over the melon, then the feta, the mint, the olives and the pine nuts.

Michael's Satanic Mushrooms

If you can have devilled eggs, you can have... Satanic Mushrooms. Michael says of his mushrooms: "I've always used the same bowl for mixing and just eyeballed everything while singing 'I don't care, I don't care!' The 13 (messy) dashes of Tabasco are ritually significant in order to attain the proper level of evil."

Serves 6

1/2 cup	miso, light or dark	120 mL
1/2 cup	dry white vermouth	120 mL
6	cloves garlic, minced	6
1/4 cup	hot, Asian-style chili sauce	60 mL
1 Tbsp.	sugar	15 mL
5 Tbsp.	dark soy sauce	75 mL
5 Tbsp.	rice wine or white wine vinegar	75 mL
1 Tbsp.	black pepper	15 mL
13	dashes Tabasco or other hot pepper sauce	13
1/4 cup	olive oil	60 mL
3 lbs.	medium-sized cultivated mushrooms, stems cut flush with the cap	1.4 kg

In a medium-sized bowl, mash the miso to a paste. Stir in the vermouth, garlic, chili sauce, sugar, soy sauce, vinegar, pepper, Tabasco sauce and olive oil. Place the mushrooms in a large plastic container with a lid and pour the marinade over the mushrooms. Cover with the lid and shake the mushrooms to distribute the marinade evenly. Refrigerate for 6 hours, shaking the mushrooms every 2 hours.

Soak the bamboo skewers in water for 30 minutes.

Heat the barbecue to medium. Skewer the mushrooms, cap to stem end, tightly on the skewers, covering the skewers completely. Grill the mushrooms slowly, turning and basting with the marinade until they are tender, 10-15 minutes.

Portobello Mushroom "Pizzas"

Portobello mushrooms are in the limelight— on polenta, grilled on salads, as a burger and on and on. Their size, flavor and texture make them an ideal palette to work with. Serve as a main course with polenta or a salad, or cut into wedges as an hors d'oeuvre. Feel free to substitute your favorite pizza ingredients.

Serves 4

4	large portobello mushrooms, about 1 1/2 bs. (680 g)	4
2	large eggs	2
1 Tbsp.	water	15 mL
1/2 cup	all-purpose flour seasoned with salt and pepper to taste	120 mL
1 cup	cornmeal	240 mL
4 Tbsp.	olive oil	60 mL
1 cup	tomato sauce	240 mL
8	thin slices prosciutto, cut crosswise into thin strips	8
1/4 cup	fresh basil leaves, coarsely chopped	60 mL
1	green onion, thinly sliced	1
1 cup	grated fontina cheese	240 mL

Remove the stems from the mushrooms. Place the eggs in a shallow bowl and beat well with the water. Place the seasoned flour and cornmeal on separate plates. Dip each mushroom in the flour, then the eggs, then the cornmeal, coating both sides with each ingredient. Place on a plate sprinkled generously with cornmeal for 5-30 minutes.

Preheat the broiler to high. Transfer the mushrooms to a baking sheet, stem side up, and brush with half the olive oil. Broil 4 inches (10 cm) away from the heat until golden brown. Turn over, brush with the remaining olive oil and broil on the other side until browned. Turn the mushrooms over again and spread each with 1/4 cup (60 mL) tomato sauce. Evenly top each with the prosciutto, basil, green onion and cheese. Place under the broiler until the cheese is bubbling and golden brown in spots.

Lovely Lemon Potatoes

These potatoes are equally good with fish or meat. If you like, they can be sprinkled with freshly grated Parmesan cheese and broiled until browned.

Serves 4

3 Tbsp.	olive oil	45 mL
2 lbs.	large russet potatoes, peeled and cut into 6 wedges each	900 g
1/2 cup	onion, finely chopped	120 mL
1/4 cup	freshly squeezed lemon juice	60 mL
1/2 cup	water or stock	120 mL
1/2 tsp.	salt	2.5 mL
1 Tbsp.	fresh parsley, finely chopped	15 mL

In a large, preferably nonstick frying pan, heat the olive oil over medium-high heat. Add the potatoes and sauté until lightly browned on one side. Turn over, scatter with the onion and sauté until browned on the other side. Turn the heat to low, add the lemon juice, water or stock and salt. Cover and cook until the potatoes are tender, turning once and adding a bit of water if the potatoes are too dry. Sprinkle with the parsley and serve immediately.

Lemon Roasted Sweet Potatoes

The lemon balances the sweetness of the potatoes.

Serves 4

4	medium unpeeled sweet potatoes, cut in half lengthwise, then into 1-inch (2.5-cm) pieces	4
1	lemon, thinly sliced and seeded	1
3	small sprigs fresh rosemary, torn into 1-inch (2.5-cm) pieces	3
1/2 tsp.	salt	2.5 mL
2 Tbsp.	olive oil	30 mL
2 Tbsp.	freshly grated Parmesan cheese	30 mL

Preheat the oven to 400°F (200°C). Combine and toss the potatoes, lemon, rosemary, salt and olive oil. Lay out in a single layer on a baking sheet. Bake for 40-45 minutes, until the potatoes are tender, turning once halfway through. Remove from the oven and toss with the Parmesan cheese.

Spaghetti with Broccoli "Pot Pesto"

If you like crunchy green broccoli, read no further. The broccoli disintegrates during the cooking and enrobes the pasta in a "creamy" green sauce.

Serves 4

2 lbs.	broccoli	900 g
4 Tbsp.	olive oil	60 mL
4	cloves garlic, minced	4
2	anchovies, chopped	2
1 lb.	good-quality spaghetti	454 g
	salt and pepper to taste	
1/2 cup	Parmesan cheese	120 mL
2 Tbsp.	pine nuts, toasted	30 mL
2 Tbsp.	fresh basil leaves, shredded	30 mL

Cut the florets from the broccoli and coarsely chop. Peel the stems and finely chop.

Bring a large pot of water to a boil and salt it generously. It should taste like seawater.

In a small saucepan, heat the olive oil over medium heat. Add the garlic and anchovies and cook until the garlic just turns golden. Remove from the heat.

Add the spaghetti and broccoli to the boiling water. Cook until the pasta is just tender to the tooth. Drain, saving 1/2 cup (120 mL) of the cooking water. Return to the pot and add the garlic mixture. Toss over low heat to coat the pasta with the mixture. Add the reserved cooking water and toss again. Check the seasoning and add salt and pepper to suit your taste. Toss with the Parmesan, pine nuts and basil and serve in heated bowls.

Penne with Beets, Bacon and Blue Cheese

This is a favorite combination—sweet, savory and sharp.

Serves 4

2	bunches walnut-sized beets, with greens, about 10 in total	2
1/4 lb.	good-quality slab bacon, cut into 1/4-inch (.6-cm) dice	113 g
4	cloves garlic, minced	4
4 Tbsp.	olive oil	60 mL
1 lb.	dry penne	454 g
4 Tbsp.	blue cheese, crumbled	60 mL
	salt and pepper to taste	

Trim and peel the beets. Discard the stems and wash the greens. Cut the greens into thin strips and cut the beets into 1/4-inch (.6-cm) dice.

Cook the bacon over low heat until it is crisp. Remove from the pan with a slotted spoon to drain on absorbent paper. Discard the bacon fat. Add the garlic and olive oil to the same pan. Cook over medium heat until the garlic is pale gold. Add the bacon and remove from the heat.

Bring a large pot of water to a boil. Add the beets to the boiling water and salt liberally. It should taste like seawater. Cook for 10 minutes. Add the penne and cook, stirring occasionally, until the pasta is very firm, about 6 minutes. Add the beet greens and continue cooking until the pasta is tender but still firm to the bite, 3-4 minutes longer. Drain the pasta and return to the pot. Add the bacon and garlic mixture and stir over low heat to coat the pasta with the sauce. Stir in the blue cheese. Season with salt and pepper. Serve immediately in heated bowls.

Corn Risotto

Good with chicken or pork or just by itself.

Serves 2 as a main course, 4 as a side dish

3 cups	fresh corn kernels, about 4 ears	720 mL
4-5 cups	chicken or vegetable stock	950-1200 mL
4 Tbsp.	unsalted butter	60 mL
2 Tbsp.	shallots, finely chopped	30 mL
1 cup	arborio rice	240 mL
1/2 cup	dry white wine	120 mL
	salt and pepper to taste	
1/3 cup	freshly grated Parmesan cheese	80 mL

Preheat the oven to 450°F (230°C). Place 1 cup (240 mL) of the corn on a baking sheet and roast for 15-20 minutes, stirring occasionally, until spotted with brown. Set aside.

Place the stock in a pot and bring to a simmer. In a large pot, melt the butter over medium heat. Add the shallots and cook, stirring until they are translucent. Add the rice and stir for a minute to coat it with the butter. Add the white wine and stir until the wine is absorbed and the rice is creamy. Continue stirring, adding the hot stock by half-cups until the rice is very firm. Season with salt and pepper and add the roasted and fresh corn. Continue adding stock until the rice is tender, creamy and slightly firm to the bite. Adjust the seasoning and stir in the Parmesan cheese.

Romano Bean Soup with Pasta

I love to eat this soup when it's cold outside. With a good bread, it makes a perfect meal. Parmesan rinds are what is left when you can grate no more cheese from a piece of Parmesan. They are a great addition to almost any soup. Save the rinds in the freezer.

Serves 6-8

3/4 cup	dried Romano beans or 1 28-oz (796-mL) can Romano beans	180 mL
1/2 cup	carrots, finely chopped	120 mL
1/2 cup	onion, finely chopped	120 mL
1/2 cup	celery, finely chopped	120 mL
2	medium cloves garlic, minced	2
2 Tbsp.	olive oil	30 mL
10 cups	chicken or beef stock	2.4 L
1	28-oz (796-mL) can tomatoes, drained and sieved	1
1	slice prosciutto, 1/4-inch (.6-cm) thick	1
1	Parmesan rind	1
	salt and pepper to taste	
1/2 lb.	short, tubular, dried pasta	227 g

If you are using dried beans, place them in a large pot and cover with water. Bring to a boil and skim off any foam that rises to the top. Turn down to a simmer and cook until tender, about 2 hours. Drain. If you are using canned beans, drain well and rinse under cold water.

In a large heavy pot over medium heat, sauté the chopped carrots, onion, celery and garlic in the olive oil until lightly browned. Add the stock, tomatoes, prosciutto and Parmesan rind. Simmer for 1 hour. Season lightly with salt. Add the beans and cook for 1 hour longer. The soup should be thick. Season with salt and pepper.

Bring a large pot of water to a boil. Add the pasta and salt liberally. It should taste like seawater. Cook, stirring occasionally, until the pasta is tender but still firm to the bite, 8-10 minutes. Drain and stir into the soup. Serve immediately in heated bowls.

Strawberries with Molasses Crème Fraîche

Another simple fruit dessert that is unique and delicious. Serve with gingersnap cookies.

Serves 4

2 pints	strawberries	950 mL
1/4 cup	orange juice	60 mL
1 Tbsp.	sugar	15 mL
1 cup	crème fraîche (page 205) or sour cream	240 mL
1/4 tsp.	vanilla	1.2 mL
4 Tbsp.	molasses	60 mL

Quickly wash and dry the strawberries. Hull and quarter them. Place in a bowl and add the orange juice and sugar. Stir gently to mix. Let stand for 10 minutes.

Mix the crème fraîche or sour cream, vanilla and molasses together. Place the strawberries in wine glasses or dessert dishes. Drizzle the crème fraîche over the top and serve.

Rosemary Crème Anglaise

This is great with fresh raspberries, blackberries, pears or peaches.

Makes 2 cups (475 mL)

2 cups	half-and-half cream	475 mL
1 Tbsp.	fresh rosemary leaves, coarsely chopped	15 mL
1	2-inch (5-cm) piece cinnamon stick	1
1/4 cup	granulated sugar	60 mL
4	extra large egg yolks	4

Combine the cream, rosemary, cinnamon stick and sugar in a large pot. Bring to a boil over high heat. Beat the egg yolks until well combined. With the cream at a rolling boil, slowly whisk it into the egg yolks. Strain through a sieve and refrigerate, whisking occasionally until cool.

Grape Cobbler

Serve this cobbler warm, with Rosemary Crème Anglaise, page 145.

Serves 6-8

1 cup	red seedless grapes	240 mL
1 cup	green seedless grapes	240 mL
1 cup	black seedless grapes	240 mL
3/4 cup	brown sugar	180 mL
2 Tbsp.	grappa or brandy	30 mL
1 Tbsp.	lemon juice	15 mL
1/2 tsp.	cinnamon	2.5 mL
1/2 cup	sliced almonds	120 mL
1 1/2 cups	all-purpose flour	360 mL
1 cup	granulated sugar	240 mL
1/4 tsp.	salt	1.2 mL
2 tsp.	lemon zest, finely chopped	10 mL
1 tsp.	fresh rosemary leaves, finely chopped	5 mL
2	eggs, lightly beaten	2
1/2 cup	milk	120 mL
4 Tbsp.	unsalted butter, melted	60 mL
2 tsp.	baking powder	10 mL
1 tsp.	vanilla	5 mL

Preheat the oven to 350°F (175°C). Generously butter a 9- by 13-inch (23- by 33-cm) baking dish.

In a medium-sized bowl combine the grapes, brown sugar, grappa, lemon juice, cinnamon and sliced almonds.

In a large bowl combine the flour, sugar, salt, lemon zest, rosemary, eggs, milk, melted butter, baking powder and vanilla. Whisk together until smooth. Do not overmix.

Pour the batter into the buttered baking dish, then evenly spread the grape mixture over the batter. Bake for 40 minutes, until a cake tester comes out clean.

Apple Cake with Warm Honey Sauce

Choose a fragrant honey for the sauce of this simple cake. It makes all the difference.

Makes 1 9- by 13-inch (23- by 33-cm) pan

3 cups	flour	720 mL
1 1/2 tsp.	baking soda	7.5 mL
1 tsp.	cinnamon	5 mL
1/4 tsp.	salt	1.2 mL
1/4 tsp.	grated nutmeg	1.2 mL
3/4 cup	vegetable oil	180 mL
1/4 cup	unsalted butter, melted	60 mL
1 cup	granulated sugar	240 mL
1 cup	dark brown sugar, packed	240 mL
3	large eggs	3
2 tsp.	pure vanilla extract	10 mL
3	large apples, peeled, cored and thinly sliced	3
1 cup	honey	240 mL
1/2 cup	unsalted butter	120 mL
1/2 cup	whipping cream	120 mL
	pinch of salt	

Preheat the oven to 350°F (175°C). Butter and flour a 9- by 13-inch (23- by 33-cm) baking pan.

Combine the flour, baking soda, cinnamon, salt and nutmeg in a large bowl. Stir well with a whisk. In another large bowl, beat the oil, butter, sugars, eggs and vanilla together with a whisk until light. Beat in the flour mixture until smooth, then fold in the apples. Pour into the prepared pan and smooth the top. Bake for 45-50 minutes, until a cake tester comes out clean. Remove to a rack to cool in the pan.

To make the honey sauce, combine the honey, butter, cream and salt in a heavy pot. Bring to a boil, stirring occasionally, and boil for 1 minute. Serve warm over the cake.

Cornmeal Pudding with Dried Blueberries

An exquisite cool-weather dessert served with a dollop of whipped cream. Use dried cranberries, cherries or a mixture of all three if you like.

Serves 6

1/4 cup	dark brown sugar, packed	60 mL
1/4 cup	fragrant honey	60 mL
1/4 cup	table molasses (not blackstrap or unsulphured)	60 mL
4 1/2 cups	milk	1070 mL
2 Tbsp.	unsalted butter	30 mL
1/2 tsp.	ground cinnamon	2.5 mL
2/3 cup	fine ground cornmeal	160 mL
2	eggs, beaten	2
1 tsp.	pure vanilla extract	5 mL
1 cup	dried blueberries	240 mL

Preheat the oven to 325°F (165°C). Butter an 8-inch-square (20-cm) noncorrodible baking dish.

Combine the brown sugar, honey, molasses, milk and butter in a large, heavy pot. Bring to a boil, stirring frequently. Slowly add the cinnamon and cornmeal. Turn the heat to low and stir constantly until thickened, about 2 minutes. Remove from the heat and quickly beat in the eggs and vanilla, then stir in the blueberries. Pour into the buttered baking dish. Place in a larger pan and pour enough hot water in the outer pan so that it comes halfway up the baking dish. Bake in the center of the oven for 70-80 minutes, until a knife inserted in the center comes out clean. Serve warm.

Orange and Pink Grapefruit Gratin with Sabayon

Sometimes simple is best. Use sweet blood oranges when they are in season in combination with the navel oranges and grapefruit. The gratin may be cooked in individual dishes for a fancy celebration.

Serves 4

1	medium pink grapefruit	1
3	large navel oranges	3
3	large egg yolks	3
1/4 cup	sugar	60 mL
1/4 cup	dry white wine	60 mL
2 Tbsp.	almond-flavored liqueur	30 mL

Peel the grapefruit and oranges with a sharp knife, removing all the white pith. Cut between the membrane and the fruit segments to release them. Remove any seeds. Arrange the segments in a shallow baking dish that holds the fruit comfortably in one layer.

In a bowl that will fit over a pot of simmering water without touching the water, whisk the egg yolks, sugar, white wine and liqueur together until well combined. Place over a pot of simmering water and whisk constantly until thickened and light in texture, about 5 minutes. If you wish to make the sabayon in advance, insert the bowl in a larger bowl filled with ice and whisk frequently until cold. Cover and refrigerate for a few hours, but not overnight.

Preheat the broiler. Spoon the sabayon over the orange and grapefruit segments. Broil until the sabayon browns on top, about 1 minute. Serve immediately.

Steamed Brown Bread with Dried Pears and Cranberries

I used to love the rich brown cakes, similar to steamed brown bread, sold in cans when I was a child. You would open both ends of the can and push the cake out. I ate it plain with butter. This is a grownup version with dried pears and cranberries, but you can omit the fruit if you like it plain. Use a 3-qt. (3-L) stainless steel bowl, 2 8-cup (2-L) pudding molds or my personal preference, 2 coffee cans. See Steamers and Steaming, page 25.

Serves 8

1 cup	flour, all-purpose or whole wheat	240 mL
1 cup	rye flour	240 mL
1 cup	cornmeal	240 mL
2 tsp.	baking soda	10 mL
1 tsp.	salt	5 mL
1 cup	table molasses (not blackstrap or unsulphured)	240 mL
2 cups	buttermilk	475 mL
3/4 cup	dried pears, finely chopped	180 mL
1/2 cup	dried cranberries	120 mL

Butter the molds you have chosen. Fill half of a steamer bottom or a pot with water and bring to a boil. If you are using a pot, place a trivet in the bottom.

Into a large bowl, sift the flours, cornmeal, baking soda and salt. Mix the molasses and buttermilk together, add to the dry ingredients and mix until just smooth. Stir in the pears and cranberries and pour evenly into the prepared molds. Cover tightly with aluminum foil or lids and place in the steamer or pot. Cover with a lid and turn the heat down to a simmer. Replenish the water with more boiling water as necessary. Check smaller molds after 2 hours and large ones after 3 hours. A toothpick inserted in the center will come out clean when the bread is done.

Remove the breads from the steamer and cool on a rack for 5 minutes before removing from the mold. Cool completely before slicing with a serrated knife.

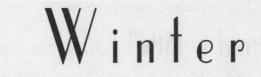

Winter

Feast of the Snow Crab

Cooked and Chilled Dungeness Crab

Lemon Mayonnaise

*M*y husband, Steven, suffers from pre-Christmas blues and wanted something festive for dinner. Veal was mentioned as a possibility, but I would have to drive halfway across town to get it. I opted for crab, which was only two blocks away. It was Christmas Eve and there were waist-high drifts of snow in the backyard. This is very unusual for Vancouver—it might happen every 60 years or so.

The crab was cooked and taken from the pot. We decided to have them chilled and I had prepared a lemony mayonnaise. A moment of madness possessed us and we ran out to the backyard with a flashlight to place the crabs in the snow. We almost choked we were laughing so hard, and the dog Ginger couldn't figure out whether to wag or sulk. We watched the crabs steaming serenely in the snow, in the weak spotlight made by the flashlight, and were awed by the reverence of the occasion. Snow Crab was born and Steven's funk disappeared!

It may never snow like that on Christmas Eve here again, but we will continue to eat Snow Crab whenever we feel in need of it. If you don't have a snowbank, the fridge will do.

Chilled crab is an easy way to eat crab. Extracting a small mountain of meat and piling it onto a piece of toasted baguette with a slathering of fresh lemon mayonnaise is one of the moments that life is all about. You can take your time with it and not worry about it getting cold. Large crabs, 1 3/4-2 lbs. (800-900 g) are ideal as there is a bigger meat reward for the amount of cracking required.

Cooked and Chilled Dungeness Crab

Choose 1 crab per person. Have your fish merchant tear off the backs and clean out the insides for you. You will not need the backs, unless you want to cook them and place them back on top for presentation. When you get home, check the crabs to make sure the lungs (these are the spongy "fingers" on the top of the body) have been removed, and rinse under cold water. Bring a pot of water that is large enough to hold the crabs to a boil. Salt liberally. It should taste like seawater. Add the crabs and cook for 5 minutes after the water comes to a boil. Remove from the pot and cool. Refrigerate for at least 1 hour until thoroughly chilled. The crab is best eaten as soon as possible. Do not refrigerate overnight.

Lemon Mayonnaise

If using raw eggs makes you uncomfortable, stir the lemon juice into 1 1/4 cups (300 mL) prepared mayonnaise.

Makes 1 1/3 cups (320 mL)

3	large egg yolks	3
1/2 tsp.	salt	2.5 mL
1/2 cup	olive oil	120 mL
1/2 cup	vegetable oil	120 mL
2 Tbsp.	lemon juice	30 mL

Place the egg yolks and salt in a food processor or blender. With the motor on, slowly dribble the olive and vegetable oils into the egg yolks. If the mixture seems too thick at any point, add a bit of water. When all of the oil has been incorporated and the mixture is emulsified, add the lemon juice. To make by hand, whisk the egg yolks and salt together in a medium-sized bowl. Whisking constantly, add the oils drop by drop until it is all incorporated and the mixture is emulsified. Whisk in the lemon juice. Cover and refrigerate for up to 3 days.

A Small Feast for
the Twelfth Day of Rain

Braised Savoy Cabbage with Meatballs

Semolina Gnocchi Casserole

Chocolate and Honey Mousse

What do you do when you can't stand the dreariness any more? Why, cook something, of course, for yourself and a select, special few. This is the time of year when comfort food really comes into play. We all have our favorites, and one of mine just happens to be this succulent dish of meatballs with cabbage. In fact, you really don't need anything with it but bread, but the other two dishes make it seem like more of a celebration. Other winter favorites are Sausages with Polenta and Porcini Mushrooms, page 185, Chicken Stew in the Style of Fish Soup, page 174, and Romano Bean Soup with Pasta, page 144. Matzoh-ball soup is way up there, and for a real quick fix, take-out barbecue duck congee from a Chinese restaurant. Whatever it is, it should give off a lot of steam and be served in a bowl so you can lift it up to your face and inhale all of the comforting goodness.

Braised Savoy Cabbage with Meatballs

I like to double the meatballs in this recipe. They make fantastic sand- wiches, pizzas and pastas. If you've eaten all the meatballs and have some cabbage left over, it can be thinned out to make a very good soup with the addition of some cooked pinto beans, small pasta shapes, or both!

Serves 4-6

1	1-inch-thick (2.5-cm) slice of good white bread, crust removed	1
1/3 cup	milk	80 mL
1/2 lb.	ground beef	227 g
1/2 lb.	ground pork	227 g
2 oz.	pancetta, finely chopped	57 g
1	large egg	1
1 Tbsp.	fresh parsley, chopped	15 mL
3 Tbsp.	freshly grated Parmesan cheese	45 mL
2 Tbsp.	onion, finely chopped	30 mL
	freshly ground black pepper	
1 cup	fine, dry breadcrumbs	240 mL
2 Tbsp.	olive oil	30 mL
2	cloves garlic, minced	2
1 1/2 lbs.	Savoy cabbage, cored and thinly sliced	680 g
	salt and pepper to taste	
1 cup	canned plum tomatoes, well-drained and coarsely chopped	240 mL

Put the bread and milk in a small saucepan and turn the heat to low. When the bread has soaked up the milk, mash it to a paste and remove from the heat. Cool completely.

Combine the beef, pork, pancetta, egg, parsley, Parmesan, onion, pepper and the bread paste. Mix thoroughly. Alternatively, place the pancetta, egg, parsley, Parmesan, onion, pepper and bread paste in the work bowl of a food processor and pulse until everything is well combined.

Add to the pork and beef and mix well. Shape into meatballs about 1 1/2 inches (3.8 cm) across. Roll in the breadcrumbs.

Place on a baking sheet and brush the tops lightly with vegetable oil. Broil, turning the meatballs until they are lightly browned on all sides.

Heat the olive oil over medium heat in a wide pot or frying pan. Sauté the garlic until golden. Add the cabbage and stir for a moment. Turn the heat down to low and cover the pan. Cook the cabbage, stirring occasionally, until it is very soft and reduced by 1/3 of its original mass, about 1 hour. If the cabbage seems in danger of burning at any point, add a bit of water.

Season with salt and pepper. Turn the heat to medium, and with the pan uncovered cook the cabbage until it is colored a light nut brown. Add the chopped tomatoes and cook for 10 minutes, stirring occasionally. Tuck the meatballs under the cabbage. Turn the heat to low. Cover and cook for 15-20 minutes.

Semolina Gnocchi Casserole

Serves 4-6

4 cups	milk	950 mL
1 1/4 cups	semolina	300 mL
4 Tbsp.	unsalted butter	60 mL
1/2 cup	freshly grated Parmesan cheese	120 mL
2 tsp.	salt	10 mL
2	egg yolks	2

There is potato gnocchi, which requires an expert's touch, gnocchi Parisienne, which is made out of poached creampuff dough, and semolina gnocchi, the easiest to make. I have made it even easier by turning it into a casserole. Semolina is a wheat product, similar to cream of wheat but a bit finer. It can be found in well-stocked supermarkets, Italian delis and natural food stores.

Butter a 9- by 13-inch (23- by 33-cm) baking dish. In a large heavy pot, heat the milk until it is almost boiling. Turn the heat to low and slowly whisk in the semolina. Using a wooden spoon, continue stirring until very thick and smooth, about 10 minutes.

Remove from the heat and beat in half the butter, half the Parmesan cheese, the salt and egg yolks. Pour into the buttered baking dish and cool. It will be thin. Score the casserole with a small knife into a crosshatch pattern. It can be prepared to this point a day in advance. Cool, cover and refrigerate. Bring to room temperature before proceeding.

Preheat the oven to 500°F (260°C). Dot the casserole with the remaining butter and sprinkle with the remaining Parmesan cheese. Bake for 15 minutes, until it has puffed up and turned a light golden color on top.

Chocolate and Honey Mousse

*F*ragrant honey contains the flavor and aroma of the flowers the bees have fed on. It usually comes from small rural producers and some really interesting ones come from other countries.

Sticky Tip

When measuring honey, molasses, corn syrup or any sticky liquid, oil your measuring utensils or use a nonstick spray. The ingredient you are measuring will literally fall right out.

Serves 6-8

2 1/2 cups	whipping cream	600 mL
12 oz.	bittersweet chocolate, chopped into small pieces	340 g
5 Tbsp.	fragrant honey	75 mL

In a heavy-bottomed pot, bring 1 cup (240 mL) of the cream to a boil. Remove from the heat and add the chocolate and honey. Stir until the chocolate is completely melted. Scrape into a large bowl and cool, stirring occasionally.

Beat 1 cup (240 mL) of the cream until soft peaks form. Fold into the cooled chocolate mixture. Divide among six 1-cup (240-mL) ramekins, wine glasses or tea cups. Chill for at least 2 hours or overnight.

Beat the remaining 1/2 cup (120 mL) cream to soft peaks. Place a small dollop on each mousse before serving.

Christmas Feast

Oxtails Braised in Red Wine

Winter Vegetable Casserole

"Drowned" Broccoli

Sweet Potatoes with Candied Ginger

Oyster Stuffing

Christmas Pie

I know that turkey is one of the symbols of holiday celebrations (I can hear my mother's voice of the past here, "Why do you always have to be different?"), but let's face it: turkey can be a complete pain. You have to be ready when the turkey is ready, it takes up all your oven space, you have to make gravy, the breast is usually dry, it has to be carved, it rarely stays hot. I am not anti-turkey, I just prefer to have it at a less hectic time of year. The oxtails can be made a few days in advance and reheated gently before serving, leaving you free to concentrate on side dishes and dessert. It is easy to double or triple the recipe for a large crowd. If you have my first book, *Pacific Passions,* Aunt Toni's Steamed Cranberry Pudding with Eggnog Sauce is an excellent finale, instead of (or with!) the Christmas pie.

One of the beauties of this meal is that the oxtails, sweet potatoes, vegetable casserole and stuffing will stay hot because of their density.

Oxtails Braised in Red Wine

I am picky about oxtails on one point—they have to be cut through the joint, not sawed into segments. You are probably not as dogmatic as I am about certain things pertaining to food and you should be relieved about that. I use whole oxtails that I buy at a Chinese butcher shop, and a heavy knife. I locate the joints and cut right through them. If you feel adventurous enough to try this, use 2 oxtails for the recipe. If not, buy 5 lbs. (2.25 kg) of cut oxtails.

Serves 6-8

1/4 cup	olive oil	60 mL
1 cup	onion, finely diced	240 mL
1/2 cup	carrot, finely diced	120 mL
1/2 cup	celery, finely diced	120 mL
1 Tbsp.	minced garlic	15 mL
2 Tbsp.	fresh parsley, finely chopped	30 mL
5 lbs.	oxtails	2.25 kg
1	large sprig fresh rosemary or thyme	1
3 cups	dry red wine	720 mL
2 cups	beef or chicken stock	475 mL
2/3 cup	well-drained, seeded and finely chopped canned Italian plum tomatoes	160 mL
	salt and pepper to taste	

Preheat the oven to 300°F (150°C).

In a large heavy pot with a tight-fitting lid that will hold the oxtails comfortably, heat the olive oil over medium heat. Add the onion, carrot, celery, garlic and parsley. Sauté until the vegetables are lightly browned. Add the oxtails, rosemary or thyme, red wine, stock and tomatoes. If the liquid does not cover the oxtails, make it up with more stock or water. Bring to a boil and cover tightly. Place in the oven and bake for 4 hours, until the oxtails are very tender but not falling apart. Check occasionally to make sure the liquid has not evaporated. Add water if the level falls below the oxtails.

Transfer the oxtails to a serving dish. Cover and place in the oven to keep warm. Skim the fat from the liquid and boil over high heat until the liquid thickens slightly, 5-8 minutes. Season with salt and pepper and pour over the oxtails. If you are making the dish in advance, transfer the oxtails to a storage container and pour the sauce over them. Cool, cover and refrigerate for up to 3 days. Gently reheat, adding a bit of water, until heated through.

Winter Vegetable Casserole

This is a good thing to eat for dinner with a green salad or steamed spinach.

Serves 6-8

1 1/2 lbs.	russet potatoes, peeled and cut into 1-inch (2.5-cm) chunks	680 g
1 1/2 lbs.	rutabaga, peeled and cut into 1-inch (2.5-cm) chunks	680 g
1	small Savoy cabbage, cut into 4 wedges, cored and cut into 1/2-inch (1.2-cm) slices	1
1/2 lb.	peeled carrots, thinly sliced	227 g
1 lb.	cream cheese, preferably natural, cut into small pieces	454 g
1/2 cup	freshly grated Parmesan cheese	120 mL
	salt and pepper to taste	
2 Tbsp.	unsalted butter	30 mL

Butter a 9- by 13-inch (23- by 33-cm) baking dish and preheat the oven to 350°F (175°C).

Place the vegetables in a large pot, cover with cold water and bring to a boil. Salt liberally. Cook until the potatoes are tender, 10-15 minutes. Drain well and return to the pot. Mash the vegetables, being concerned only that the potatoes are well mashed.

Stir in the cream cheese and Parmesan cheese and season with salt and pepper. Transfer the vegetables to the buttered baking dish and dot the top with butter. Bake for 45 minutes, until the top is lightly browned. You may prepare and refrigerate the casserole a day in advance. Remove from the fridge and bake for 1 to 1 1/4 hours until hot all the way through.

"Drowned" Broccoli

No crunchy green broccoli here, only an utterly delicious, heady, intensely flavored vegetable dish. The broccoli is drowned in red wine, hence the name.

Serves 6-8

3 lbs.	broccoli	1.4 kg
3 cups	onion, thinly sliced	720 mL
6	oil-packed anchovy filets, chopped	6
4 oz.	Parmesan cheese, slivered into thin pieces	113 g
16	brine-cured black olives, such as Kalamata, pitted and cut in half	16
1 1/2 cups	dry red wine	360 mL
1/4 cup	olive oil	60 mL

Cut the stalks from the broccoli and peel them. Cut them into 1/2-inch (1.2-cm) diagonal slices. Cut the broccoli crowns into florets.

In a large pot, place one-fourth of the broccoli, then one-third of the onion, anchovies, Parmesan cheese and olives. Continue layering in this manner, ending with broccoli. Pour the wine and olive oil over the broccoli and bring to a boil. Turn the heat to low, cover and simmer for 45 minutes. Remove the lid and increase the heat to medium. Cook until the wine has almost completely evaporated. Check the seasoning. You will probably not need any salt because of the salt in the anchovies, cheese and olives.

Sweet Potatoes with Candied Ginger

The candied ginger used in this recipe is the dry crystallized one, dusted with granulated sugar. I have a real fondness for it and like to nibble it with chocolate after dinner. Its sharpness is a great match for the silky sweet potatoes.

Serves 6-8

1/2 cup	candied ginger	120 mL
3 lbs.	sweet potatoes, peeled and cubed	1.4 kg
4 Tbsp.	unsalted butter	60 mL
1/2 cup	sour cream	120 mL
	salt and pepper to taste	

Either by hand or with a food processor, chop the ginger until it's almost puréed. Reserve.

Place the sweet potatoes in a large pot and cover with cold water. Bring to a boil and cook until the potatoes are tender, about 15 minutes. Drain and mash the potatoes by hand or purée in a food processor until smooth. Stir in the butter until melted, then the sour cream and ginger. Season with salt and pepper. The potatoes may be prepared up to 2 days in advance. Reheat over low heat, stirring frequently, until piping hot.

Oyster Stuffing

Serves 6-8

1/3 cup	unsalted butter	80 mL
2 cups	onion, finely diced	475 mL
1 cup	celery, finely diced	240 mL
2 tsp.	fresh thyme leaves	10 mL
3/4 cup	chicken stock, plus more if needed	180 mL
1 pint	shucked oysters, cut into quarters	475 mL
1 tsp.	black pepper	5 mL
8 cups	firm white bread, crusts removed, cut into 1/2-inch (1.2-cm) cubes	2 L
	salt to taste	

I only started to eat oyster stuffing when I moved to the West Coast and was sorry I hadn't had it before. Like most dishes with cooked oysters, the meat almost disappears, leaving its intense briny flavor behind. I like a lot of black pepper in this, but adjust it to your taste. You can serve it with any large roasted bird, but it is especially good with oxtails.

In a frying pan, melt the butter over low heat. Add the onion, celery and thyme. Cook until the onion is translucent. Add the chicken stock and bring to a boil. Add the oysters and pepper and remove from the heat. Pour the mixture over the bread cubes and toss well. The stuffing should be moist but not soggy. Add more chicken stock if it seems too dry. Season with salt.

Preheat the oven to 350°F (175°C). Transfer the stuffing to a 9- by 13-inch (23- by 33-cm) baking dish. Cover with aluminum foil and bake for 1/2 hour. Remove the foil and bake 15-20 minutes longer, until the top is brown and crusty.

Christmas Pie

To my taste, this leaves mincemeat in the culinary Dark Ages. Serve it with sweetened whipped cream to which you have added a bit of rum or brandy.

Makes 1 10-inch (25-cm) pie

1 cup	pitted prunes	240 mL
1 1/2 cups	boiling water	360 mL
2/3 cup	Candied Kumquats	160 mL
3 cups	apples, peeled and thinly sliced	720 mL
1 Tbsp.	flour	15 mL
2 Tbsp.	syrup from the candied kumquats	30 mL
10 oz.	marzipan	285 g
4 Tbsp.	butter	60 mL
2	eggs	2
1 recipe	Flaky Pastry (page 206)	1 recipe
1	egg yolk	1
1 Tbsp.	water	15 mL
1 Tbsp.	sugar	15 mL

Preheat the oven to 425°F (220°C).

Pour the boiling water over the prunes, cover and let stand for 10 minutes. Drain well and coarsely chop. Combine the prunes, kumquats, apples, flour and kumquat syrup. Set aside. Place the marzipan in the work bowl of a food processor and pulse a few times. Add the butter and eggs and pulse until well combined. If you're using an electric mixer, beat the marzipan on low speed for one minute. Beat in the butter until combined, then the eggs, one at a time.

Roll out the pastry into a 15-inch (38-cm) round. Fit the pastry into the pan but do not trim the excess. Spread the marzipan mixture over the bottom of the pastry, then evenly distribute the apple mixture on top. Fold the pastry over the pie, coaxing it into elegant folds. Beat the egg yolk with the water. Brush the top of the pie with the egg yolk mixture and sprinkle with the sugar. Bake in the center of the oven for 15 minutes. Reduce the heat to 350°F (175°C) and bake for another 30-40 minutes until the pastry is golden brown. Serve warm or at room temperature.

Candied Kumquats

Makes 2 1/2 cups

1 lb.	kumquats	454 g
2 cups	sugar	475 mL
1 1/2 cups	water	360 mL

Cut the kumquats in half through the middle and pick out the seeds with the point of a small knife. Combine the sugar and water in a heavy saucepan. Bring to a boil and add the kumquats. Turn down to a bare simmer and cook for 1/2 hour, until the kumquats turn darker and become translucent. Cool. The kumquats will keep indefinitely, covered and refrigerated.

Kumquats are small, oblong oranges that appear in winter. Preserved, they can be eaten skin and all; unlike oranges, the skin is not bitter. Candied kumquats can be eaten on toast or served with pork and chicken.

Salmon Baked in Red Wine with Mushrooms and Bacon

If you are lucky enough to have access to chanterelles in the fall, use them in place of cultivated mushrooms. Their woodsy flavor is a treat not to be missed.

Serves 4

1 1/2 lbs.	center-cut salmon filet, 2 inches (5 cm) thick, skin on	680 g
	salt and pepper to taste	
1/4 cup	shallots, finely diced	60 mL
1 cup	dry red wine	240 mL
1/2 lb.	slab bacon, rind removed, cut into 1/4-inch (.6-cm) dice	227 g
1 Tbsp.	unsalted butter	15 mL
3/4 lb.	mushrooms, thickly sliced	340 g
2 Tbsp.	unsalted butter	30 mL
1/4 cup	fresh parsley, finely chopped	60 mL
1	clove garlic, minced	1

Preheat the oven to 350°F (175°C). Place the salmon in a baking dish that holds it snugly. Season with salt and pepper. Scatter the shallots around the salmon and pour the red wine over all. Cover tightly with aluminum foil and bake for 30 minutes. The salmon will still be moist and pink in the middle.

While the salmon is baking, slowly render the bacon on medium heat until crisp. Drain the bacon and discard the fat. Set aside.

In a large, nonstick pan, melt the 1 Tbsp. (15 mL) butter over high heat. Add the mushrooms and sauté briskly until lightly browned. Remove from the heat.

Remove the salmon from the oven. Transfer the filet to a plate, cover and keep warm. Add the red wine and shallots to the mushrooms. Boil over high heat until the wine is syrupy. Add the bacon and remove from the heat. Whisk in the 2 Tbsp. (30 mL) butter, stirring constantly. Check for seasoning.

Mix the parsley and garlic together. Cut the salmon into four pieces and transfer to heated plates. Spoon the sauce over the salmon and sprinkle with the parsley and garlic.

Baked Mackerel with Smoked Chorizo Sausage

Unfortunately for me, few people share my love of mackerel. It is a wonderful fish, well salted, grilled and served with lemon or with Caponata, page 91. Its availability is greater in the east, no doubt due to the larger Portuguese and Italian population there. Smoked chorizo sausages are a spicy Portuguese sausage. I like to use their flavor as a seasoning, much the same way I would use prosciutto, pancetta or bacon.

Serves 4

2 Tbsp.	olive oil	30 mL
1 cup	drained, canned plum tomatoes, finely chopped	240 mL
1/4 cup	sweet yellow pepper, finely diced	60 mL
1/4 cup	sweet red pepper, finely diced	60 mL
1/2 cup	onion, finely diced	120 mL
2	cloves garlic, minced	2
1/4 tsp.	salt	1.2 mL
1/2 cup	smoked chorizo sausage, finely diced	120 mL
2 lbs.	small mackerel, approximately 8 fish	900 g
1 Tbsp.	balsamic vinegar	15 mL
2 Tbsp.	fresh parsley, coarsely chopped	30 mL

Preheat the oven to 350°F (175°C).

Heat the olive oil in a large frying pan and add the tomatoes, red and yellow peppers, onion, garlic and salt. Cook over medium heat, stirring frequently, until the mixture thickens, about 5 minutes. Remove from the heat and add the chorizo.

Place the mackerel in a baking pan that will hold the fish snugly without overlapping. Spoon the tomato mixture over the fish, leaving their heads exposed. Cover the dish with aluminum foil and bake for 15 minutes. Uncover the dish and bake for 15 minutes longer. Remove from the oven and drizzle with the balsamic vinegar and sprinkle with the chopped parsley. Serve hot or at room temperature.

Alaskan Black Cod with Clams and Chorizo Sausage

An extremely flavorful and sumptuous meal in a bowl. One of my favorites. This is equally good with sea bass.

Serves 4

4	1-inch (2.5-cm) slices good, sturdy bread	4
1	clove garlic, peeled	1
	olive oil	
1/2 lb.	chorizo sausage, Spanish or smoked Portuguese-style	227 g
1 cup	white wine	240 mL
1 cup	drained, canned plum tomatoes, seeded and finely chopped	240 mL
1 lb.	fresh Manila clams	454 g
4	4-oz. (113-g) filets Alaskan black cod	4
	olive oil	
	salt and pepper to taste	
1/2 cup	orzo, cooked until tender	120 mL
1/4 lb.	spinach, stems removed	113 g

Preheat the oven to 400°F (200°C). Grill or toast the bread on both sides. Rub the bread on one side with the garlic clove and drizzle with olive oil. Place one slice in each of four deep pasta bowls.

Peel the skin from the chorizo sausage and tear it into 1/2-inch (1.2-cm) pieces. Place in a pot large enough to hold the clams comfortably. Add the wine and bring to a boil. Add the tomatoes and clams. Cover with a lid and steam until the clams just open. Remove from the heat.

Place the fish on an oiled baking sheet. Brush with olive oil and season with salt and pepper. Bake for 12 minutes, or until the fish is just done. Remove from the oven and cover loosely with aluminum foil to keep warm.

Add the orzo and spinach leaves to the clam mixture. Cover and bring to a boil. Stir once or twice and remove from the heat. Place the fish on the toasted bread. Spoon the clam mixture around the fish and serve.

Prawns in Cocoa Sauce

This dish was inspired by a customer who asked me if I had ever heard of shrimp with chocolate sauce. The customer had a recipe for it years ago but lost it. I thought of Mexican moles and ancient Spanish dishes that use sweet spices and cocoa in their sauces, did some research and some cooking, and this is what I came up with. A mortar and pestle works best to pound the almonds and garlic to a paste.

Serves 3-4

3/4 lb.	large prawns	340 g
1 Tbsp.	olive oil	15 mL
1	whole dried chili pepper	1
1/4 cup	onion, finely diced	60 mL
1 cup	well-drained, canned plum tomatoes, puréed	240 mL
	and sieved to remove their seeds	
1/4 cup	red wine	60 mL
1	whole clove	1
1/2 tsp.	cocoa	2.5 mL
1/4 tsp.	salt	1.2 mL
	a large pinch of sugar	
	a large pinch of cinnamon	
10	whole skinless almonds, toasted	10
1	small clove garlic, peeled	1
2 tsp.	fresh parsley, chopped	10 mL

Peel the prawns, saving the shells. Place the shells in a pot and cover with 1 1/2 cups (360 mL) water. Bring to a boil and simmer for 20 minutes. Drain the stock, discarding the shells. Reserve 1/2 cup (120 mL) of the liquid.

Heat the olive oil in a large, nonstick frying pan over medium-low heat. Add the chili pepper and fry until it turns dark brown. Add the onion and puréed tomatoes. Cook, stirring frequently, until the tomatoes thicken, about 5 minutes. Discard the chili pepper. Add the red wine, reserved prawn stock, whole clove, cocoa, salt, sugar and cinnamon. Simmer over low heat for 5 minutes.

With a mortar and pestle, pound the almonds to a paste. Add the garlic clove and pound it to a paste. If you prefer, combine the almonds and garlic in a blender or food processor. Blend until a paste is formed, adding a few spoonfuls of the tomato sauce to help it along. Stir in the chopped parsley.

Add the prawns to the tomato mixture and cook, stirring frequently, until the prawns are cooked through, about 3-4 minutes. Stir in the almond mixture and serve.

Oyster Pie

A fine and comforting dish for a cold day.

Serves 4

1/2 lb.	fresh spinach, stems removed, washed	227 g
2 Tbsp.	unsalted butter	30 mL
1 cup	onion, finely diced	240 mL
1/2 cup	fennel bulb, finely diced	120 mL
1 cup	dry white wine	240 mL
2 cups	whipping cream	475 mL
1 tsp.	salt	5 mL
2 tsp.	fresh tarragon, finely chopped	10 mL
1 Tbsp.	fresh lemon juice	15 mL
2 1/2 lbs.	russet potatoes, peeled and cut into 1-inch (2.5-cm) chunks	1.1 kg
1/2 cup	buttermilk, warmed	120 mL
2 Tbsp.	unsalted butter at room temperature	30 mL
1 Tbsp.	prepared horseradish	15 mL
	salt and pepper to taste	
24	shucked medium oysters	24
1/2 cup	fine dry breadcrumbs	120 mL
	paprika	

In a large pot, steam the spinach, using only the water clinging to its leaves. Drain and place on a plate to cool. Squeeze the water out of the spinach and chop coarsely. Set aside.

In a large pot, melt the butter over medium heat. Add the onion and fennel and sauté until the onion is translucent. Add the white wine, turn the heat to high and boil until the wine is reduced by half. Add the whipping cream and boil until the mixture is reduced to 1 1/2 cups (360 mL). Stir in the salt, tarragon and lemon juice. Remove from the heat.

Cover the potatoes with water, bring to a boil and cook until the potatoes are very tender, 15-20 minutes. Drain and return to the pot. Mash the potatoes until smooth. Beat in the buttermilk, then the butter and horseradish. Season with salt and pepper.

Preheat the oven to 425°F (220°C). Place the oysters in an 8-inch-square (20-cm) baking dish and sprinkle with the breadcrumbs. Stir the spinach into the sauce and pour over the oysters. Spoon the mashed potatoes over the sauce and sprinkle lightly with paprika. Place in the oven and bake for 20-30 minutes, until the mixture is bubbling and the potatoes are lightly browned.

Baked Oysters with Wasabi Mayonnaise

This is stunningly good. I got the idea after eating in Japanese restaurants where oysters and sea urchin roe were broiled under a topping of plain mayonnaise.

Serves 6 as an appetizer, 3-4 as a main course

1 cup	mayonnaise (commercially prepared)	240 mL
1 Tbsp.	prepared wasabi paste	15 mL
24	freshly shucked oysters on the half-shell	24
1 Tbsp.	toasted sesame seeds	15 mL
2	green onions, finely chopped	2

Combine the mayonnaise and wasabi paste until well blended.

Choose a large, rimmed pan to cook the oysters on. Crumple a piece of aluminum foil twice as large as the pan you are using to broil the oysters in and then stretch it out to fit the pan. You want the little hills and valleys of the foil to hold the oysters securely, so don't smooth it out. Spread about 1 tsp. (5 mL) of the mayonnaise over each oyster, sprinkle with the sesame seeds and arrange on the pan. The oysters may be prepared up to an hour in advance. Cover and refrigerate.

Preheat the broiler. Broil the oysters until the mayonnaise picks up brown spots, 3-4 minutes. Sprinkle with the green onion and serve on the half-shell.

Baked Oysters with Chipotle Chilies

Oysters are delicious with this smoky, spicy topping. Chipotle chilies have become deservedly more popular over the past few years, and you see them used mostly in sauces. Chipotle chilies are ripe jalapeño peppers that have been dried and smoked. They can be bought loose and dried or bought pickled (en adobo) in cans like the ones used in this recipe. Well-stocked supermarkets and Latin American food stores carry them.

Serves 6 as an appetizer, 3-4 as a main course

1	7 1/2-oz. (213-mL) can pickled chipotle chilies	1
2 Tbsp.	vegetable oil	30 mL
3	cloves garlic, minced	3
2 tsp.	ground coriander seeds	10 mL
1/4 tsp.	dried oregano	1.2 mL
	pinch of ground cloves	
1/2	avocado, finely chopped	1/2
2 tsp.	freshly squeezed lime juice	10 mL
	salt and pepper to taste	
24	freshly shucked oysters on the half-shell	24
2 Tbsp.	olive oil	30 mL
24	fresh coriander leaves	24

In a food processor or blender, combine the chipotle chilies, vegetable oil, garlic, coriander seeds, oregano and cloves. Process until almost smooth. If making it by hand, chop the chilies until pasty. Transfer the chilies to a bowl and stir in the other ingredients.

Combine the avocado and lime juice. Season with salt and pepper. Set aside.

Choose a large, rimmed pan to cook the oysters on. Crumple a piece of aluminum foil twice as large as the pan you are using to broil the oysters and then stretch it out to fit the pan. You want the little hills and valleys of the foil to hold the oysters securely, so don't smooth it out. Spread about 1/4 tsp. (1.2 mL) of the paste over each oyster (or more if you like the heat), and arrange them on the pan. Drizzle each oyster with olive oil. The oysters may be prepared up to an hour in advance. Cover and refrigerate.

Preheat the broiler. Broil the oysters for 3-4 minutes, until their edges curl. Top with a small spoonful of the avocado mixture and garnish each one with a coriander leaf. Serve hot, on the half-shell.

Oysters Baked in Garlic and Sherry for Erin

Erin's parents own a beautiful cottage where we go for mini vacations. Erin always wants oysters, so I like to make a different oyster dish every time. This received 5 stars.

Serves 4 as a main course

3/4 qt.	small, shucked oysters	720 mL
1 cup	unsalted butter	240 mL
1/3 cup	sweet sherry	80 mL
4	cloves garlic, minced	4
1/4 tsp.	salt	1.2 mL
2 tsp.	coarsely crushed black pepper	10 mL
6 cups	breadcrumbs (use day-old white bread)	1.5 L

Preheat the oven to 400°F (200°C). Place the oysters in a single layer in a 9- by 13-inch (23- by 33-cm) baking dish. In a pot over low heat, melt the butter. Add the sherry, garlic, salt and pepper. Add the breadcrumbs and toss until well coated. Spread the breadcrumbs evenly over the oysters. Do not pack them down. Bake for 20 minutes in the middle of the oven. Turn on the broiler and broil until the top is golden brown, 3-4 minutes.

Clams with Bacon, Olives and Tomatoes

I love this heady combination of flavors with the smoothness of the cream. Add some boiled, sliced potatoes to the cooking pot for an exotic chowder. You may omit the whipping cream if you prefer.

Serves 4

1/2 lb.	sliced bacon, cut into 1/2-inch (1.2-cm) pieces	227 g
4	cloves garlic, minced	4
1/4 cup	shallots, finely chopped	60 mL
1/2 cup	dry white wine	120 mL
1/2 cup	drained, canned plum tomatoes, finely chopped	120 mL
12	large, quality green olives, pitted and chopped	12
1/2 cup	whipping cream or crème fraîche (page 205)	120 mL
3 lbs.	Manila clams, scrubbed	1.4 kg
2 Tbsp.	fresh parsley, finely chopped	30 mL

In a large pot, cook the bacon on low heat until crisp. Remove the bacon and discard all the fat except 1 Tbsp. (15 mL). Turn the heat to high and add the garlic and shallots. When they sizzle, add the wine, tomatoes, olives, whipping cream or crème fraîche and clams. Cover tightly and steam until the clams open, shaking the pot occasionally. When the clams have opened, add the bacon and parsley and shake to mix. Serve in heated bowls.

Chicken Stew in the Style of Fish Soup

This dish is based on bouillabaisse, the Provençal fish stew flavored with tomatoes, saffron and fennel, and enriched with aioli, a garlic mayonnaise. These flavors go equally well with chicken, and it's much less intimidating than making a bouillabaisse.

Serves 4-6

2 Tbsp.	olive oil	30 mL
2 lbs.	bone-in chicken breasts, cut in quarters	900 g
2 lbs.	bone-in chicken thighs	900 g
1 cup	onion, finely diced	240 mL
3	large leeks, white and light green part only, thinly sliced (see A Bit About Leeks, page 191)	3
2/3 cup	fresh fennel bulb, finely diced	160 mL
4	cloves garlic, minced	4
3 cups	well-drained, canned plum tomatoes, finely chopped	720 mL
3 cups	chicken stock	720 mL
2 cups	dry white wine	475 mL
	large pinch of saffron threads	
2	bay leaves	2
1 tsp.	fennel seeds	5 mL
1/2 tsp.	crushed dried chilies	2.5 mL
2	small sprigs fresh thyme	2
1	strip fresh orange rind	1
	salt and pepper to taste	
1 lb.	small red potatoes, quartered	454 g
2 Tbsp.	fresh parsley, finely chopped	30 mL
6	thick slices good-quality toasted baguette	6
1 recipe	Aioli	1 recipe

In a large frying pan, heat 1 Tbsp. (15 mL) of the olive oil over medium heat. Remove the skin from the chicken if you prefer and season the chicken with salt and pepper. Cook in batches until golden brown on both sides. Transfer to a plate.

In a large heavy pot, heat the remaining olive oil over medium heat. Add the onion, leeks, fennel and garlic and cook, stirring occasionally, until the vegetables become soft but not brown, 4-5 minutes. Add the tomatoes and cook, stirring frequently, until most of the liquid has evaporated. Add the chicken stock, wine, saffron, bay leaves, fennel, chili, thyme, orange rind and the chicken pieces with any liquid on the plate. Season lightly with salt and pepper. Cover and simmer over low heat for 35-40 minutes, until the chicken is tender and cooked through. Transfer the chicken to a plate and remove any fat accumulated on top of the liquid. Boil over high heat for 5 minutes. Return the chicken to the pot and remove from the heat.

While the chicken is cooking, cook the potatoes. Place the potatoes in a pot and cover with cold salted water by a few inches (8 cm). Bring to a boil and cook until the potatoes are tender, 10-15 minutes. Drain and reserve.

When you are ready to serve the chicken, add the potatoes to the pot and bring to a vigorous simmer. Stir in the chopped parsley. Place a piece of toasted bread in each of 6 heated bowls. Ladle the stew into the bowls and serve with the aioli on the side.

Aioli

Traditional aioli doesn't have lemon juice in it, but I like the flavor.

Makes 1 1/3 cups (320 mL)

1/2 tsp.	salt	2.5 mL
3	cloves garlic, minced	3
3	large egg yolks	3
1 cup	olive oil	240 mL
4 tsp.	lemon juice	20 mL

In a small bowl, mash the garlic and salt to a paste with the back of a spoon. Place the egg yolks in a food processor or blender. Add the garlic paste and turn the motor on. Slowly dribble the olive oil into the egg yolks. If the mixture seems too thick at any point, add a dribble of water. When all of the oil has been incorporated and the mixture is emulsified, add the lemon juice. To make by hand, whisk the egg yolks and mashed garlic together in a medium-sized bowl. Whisking constantly, add the oil, drop by drop, until all of the oil is incorporated and the mixture is emulsified. Whisk in the lemon juice. Cover and refrigerate for up to 3 days.

Note: If using raw eggs makes you uncomfortable, stir the garlic and 2 tsp. (10 mL) lemon juice into 1 1/4 cups (300 mL) prepared mayonnaise.

Duck Legs Steamed in Red Wine with Orange, Rosemary and Prosciutto

Using steam instead of direct heat to gently braise the duck produces extremely tender, flavor-infused meat. The parsley, orange, garlic and prosciutto garnish works in harmony with the deep rich flavors of the braising liquid. I served this with spaetzle and was completely ecstatic with the results.

Serves 4

1	1/4-inch (.6-cm) slice prosciutto	1
2	medium shallots, peeled	2
4	medium cloves garlic, peeled	4
12	whole black peppercorns	12
2	allspice berries	2
1/2 tsp.	whole coriander seeds	2.5 mL
2	small sprigs fresh rosemary	2
4	duck legs, 1/2 lb. (227 g) each, or 1 large duck, 6-7 lbs. (2.8-3.2 kg), backbone removed, quartered and rib bones removed from the breast, trimmed of all fat	4
3 cups	dry red wine	720 mL
1 Tbsp.	unsalted butter, softened	15 mL
1 Tbsp.	all-purpose flour	15 mL
	salt and pepper to taste	
1 tsp.	olive oil	5 mL
3 Tbsp.	prosciutto, finely diced	45 mL
2 Tbsp.	fresh parsley, finely chopped	30 mL
1 tsp.	garlic, finely chopped	5 mL
	zest of 1/2 orange, finely chopped	
1/2 tsp.	fresh rosemary leaves, finely chopped	2.5 mL

Choose a 1 1/2-quart (1.5-L) pot or casserole dish with a lid that will hold the duck snugly and fit comfortably in the steamer. (See Steamers and Steaming, page 25.) Place the slice of prosciutto, shallots, garlic, peppercorns, allspice, coriander and rosemary in the bottom of the dish. Add the duck in a single layer and pour in the red wine. If the wine does not quite cover the duck, add water to cover by 1/2 inch (1.2 cm). Cover the pot tightly with a double thickness of aluminum foil and then cover with a lid.

Fill the steamer pot almost full with water and bring to a boil. Place the pot or casserole in the steaming basket and cover with the lid. Steam for 2 hours, replenishing with boiling water if the level becomes too low. Remove the duck pieces to a plate and cover. Skim all the fat from the top of the liquid and strain the liquid through a sieve. Reduce over high heat to half. Mix the softened butter and flour together to form a smooth paste. Whisk into the boiling sauce by teaspoonfuls until it is lightly thickened. You may not need to use all the flour paste. Season with salt and pepper and set aside.

In a small, nonstick frying pan, heat the olive oil over medium-low heat. Add the diced prosciutto and cook until it is brown and crisp, about 10 minutes. Remove the prosciutto with a slotted spoon to drain on a paper towel. Mix the parsley, garlic, orange zest, rosemary and prosciutto together. You may prepare the recipe to this point 1 or 2 hours in advance.

Preheat the broiler. Place the duck on a baking sheet and broil 4 inches (10 cm) from the heat until the skin is brown and crispy, about 5-6 minutes. While the duck is broiling, reheat the sauce. Place the duck on heated plates and pour the sauce over it. Sprinkle the prosciutto mixture over the duck and serve immediately.

Pot Roast Smothered in Onion

Chuck roasts are cheap and extremely flavorful cuts of meat. The onion provides almost all the liquid needed to cook the roast, with a little help from some red wine. Ask your butcher to net the roast to make it easier to handle. This serves a crowd and makes great leftovers.

Serves 8

2	medium carrots, sliced	2
2	leeks, white part only, cleaned and sliced	2
1	stalk celery, sliced	1
1/2	medium white onion, sliced	1/2
6	allspice berries	6
1/4 tsp.	black peppercorns	1.2 mL
12	cloves garlic, peeled and cut in half	12
5	small sprigs fresh rosemary	5
3 cups	dry red wine	720 mL
1	chuck roast, approximately 8 lbs. (3.5 kg)	1
4 Tbsp.	vegetable oil	60 mL
6 lbs.	onion, thinly sliced into half-moons	2.7 kg
2 tsp.	salt	10 mL
2 cups	sour cream	475 mL
2 Tbsp.	freshly grated horseradish or 4 Tbsp. (60 mL) prepared horseradish	30 mL
	salt and pepper to taste	
2	small sprigs fresh rosemary	2
4	whole cloves	4
1 Tbsp.	balsamic or red wine vinegar	15 mL
	salt and pepper to taste	

The day before you are going to serve the pot roast, combine the carrots, leeks, celery, onion, allspice, peppercorns, garlic, rosemary and red wine in a noncorrodible pot. Bring to a boil, turn down the heat and simmer over low heat for 5 minutes. Remove from the heat and cool completely.

Place the chuck roast in a high-sided container that will hold it snugly (I like to use a pot). Pour the red wine mixture over the beef, lifting it to ensure that some of the wine gets underneath. Cover and refrigerate overnight or up to 3 days, turning the roast over every day.

Preheat the oven to 300°F (150°C). Heat 1 Tbsp. (15 mL) of the vegetable oil in a very large frying pan over medium heat. Remove the beef from the marinade and

brown it on all sides. Remove to a plate. Add the remaining 3 Tbsp. (45 mL) oil to the pan, the onion and the 2 tsp. (10 mL) salt. Sauté the onion, stirring frequently, until it softens slightly. A bit of browning is fine.

Place the beef in a large, high-sided pot that will fit it snugly. You want the onion to completely surround the beef. If you use a large roasting pan, the onion juices will evaporate quickly, rather than create the cooking medium for the beef. Pour the red wine mixture through a sieve over the beef and onion. Cover with aluminum foil and a tight-fitting lid. Place in the oven and bake for 4 hours. Check the roast by inserting a small knife through the top of the roast. There should be little resistance. If the roast seems a bit tough, cover again and cook for another hour.

Stir the sour cream and horseradish together. Season with salt and pepper. Set aside.

Remove the pot from the oven and carefully remove the beef. Cover and keep warm. Strain the onion through a sieve, saving the rich stock. Remove the fat from the stock. Place the onion, stock, rosemary and cloves in a large pot or frying pan and cook over medium heat, stirring frequently, until the mixture thickens and turns a rich brown, about 20 minutes. Remove the rosemary sprigs and cloves. Stir in the vinegar and season with salt and pepper. Remove the net and any bones from the roast. Slice or cut the beef into chunks and place on a heated platter. Pour onion sauce over the beef. Serve with any additional onion sauce and the sour cream and horseradish on the side.

Beef Tenderloin Steaks Poached in Red Wine with Horseradish Sauce

Although poaching beef seems slightly unorthodox, it produces a very tender steak because of the gentle cooking. Serve this when you want to impress others or just yourself!

Serves 4

1/2 cup	shallots, finely chopped	120 mL
2 cups	dry red wine	475 mL
1 Tbsp.	whole black peppercorns	15 mL
2	sprigs fresh thyme	2
4	6-oz. (170-g) beef tenderloin steaks	4
1/2 cup	whipping cream	120 mL
1 Tbsp.	prepared horseradish	15 mL
	salt to taste	

In a pot large enough to hold the steaks snugly without overlapping, combine the shallots, wine, peppercorns and thyme and bring to a boil. Fit the steaks into the pot, adding water if necessary to bring the liquid 1/4 inch (.6 cm) above the steaks. Turn the heat down to a bare simmer. After 8 minutes, check one of the steaks with an instant-read thermometer. (See How Do I Know When It's Done?, page 119.) Check every 2 minutes and when the steaks are done to your liking, remove them from the poaching liquid, place them on a plate and cover with foil to keep warm.

Over high heat, reduce the liquid in the pot to 1 cup (240 mL). Add the whipping cream and continue reducing until the sauce is thickened. To test, dip a spoon in the sauce and draw your finger through the sauce on the back of the spoon. If the track of your finger remains, the sauce is ready. Strain through a sieve and return to the pot. Save a few peppercorns if you wish, to garnish the steaks. Add the horseradish and check for salt. Add the steaks and any juices to the pot. Warm over medium heat for a minute on both sides. Place on heated plates and spoon the sauce over the steaks. Serve immediately.

Hubert's Whole Roasted Veal Shanks

I never realized that you could roast veal shanks (silly me!), thinking they would be tough. Why else would they always be braised? Dinner at Hubert's proved my assumption wrong when he roasted whole shanks to a state of ultimate succulence. That plus lots and lots of delicious marrow, good company and his mother's incredible blueberry schnapps made a memorable evening. The shanks are equally good without the sauce.

Serves 6

1 cup	carrots, cut into 1/2-inch (1.2-cm) dice	240 mL
1 cup	celery, cut into 1/2-inch (1.2-cm) dice	240 mL
1/2 cup	onion, cut into 1/2-inch (1.2-cm) dice	120 mL
1	leek, white and light green part only, thinly sliced (see A Bit About Leeks, page 191)	1
6	large sprigs fresh thyme, coarsely chopped	6
1 Tbsp.	fresh parsley, finely chopped	15 mL
2	milk-fed veal shanks, 2 1/2 lbs. (1.1 kg) each	2
1 tsp.	salt	5 mL
2 Tbsp.	vegetable oil	30 mL
1 cup	white wine, heated	240 mL
3 cups	chicken stock	720 mL
1 Tbsp.	butter, softened	15 mL
1 Tbsp.	flour	15 mL

Combine the vegetables and herbs in a 9- by 13-inch (23- by 33-cm) glass baking dish. Sprinkle the veal shanks with the salt and place them in the pan, packing half the vegetables on top. Cover and refrigerate overnight.

Preheat the oven to 350°F (175°C). Heat the oil over medium heat in a large frying pan. Brown the shanks on all sides and replace on top of the vegetables in the baking dish. Roast for 1 hour. Reduce the heat to 300°F (150°C) and roast for 1 1/2 hours longer. Let the meat rest for 15 minutes. With the aid of a kitchen towel, tongs and a knife, remove the meat from the bones in one piece. Slice thinly across the grain and place on a heated platter. Serve the bones too, for those who like marrow.

To make a sauce for the shanks, pour the heated white wine into the roasting pan after you have removed the shanks, and scrape to loosen any brown bits stuck to the pan. Transfer to a pot and add the chicken stock. Bring to a boil and simmer for 10 minutes. Remove any fat that has collected on the top. Mix butter with the flour until smooth. Whisk into the sauce and cook for a few minutes longer. Strain through a sieve and season with salt and pepper. Serve on the side.

Steven's Spaghetti and Meatballs

Steven is a wonderful cook—especially of familiar and comforting things. His spaghetti and meatballs proves it.

Serves 4-6

1/3 cup	milk	80 mL
3	1-inch (2.5-cm) slices white bread, crusts removed and torn into pieces	3
1	large egg	1
1 lb.	lean ground beef	454 g
1 lb.	ground pork	454 g
1 cup	freshly grated Parmesan cheese	240 mL
1 tsp.	salt	5 mL
1/4 tsp.	pepper	1.2 mL
1/4 cup	fresh parsley, chopped	60 mL
4	28-oz. (796-mL) cans Italian plum tomatoes, drained	4
4 Tbsp.	olive oil	60 mL
3 Tbsp.	prosciutto, finely chopped	45 mL
1 Tbsp.	garlic, finely chopped	15 mL
2/3 cup	onion, finely diced	160 mL
1 Tbsp.	tomato paste	15 mL
1 tsp.	salt	5 mL
1/4 tsp.	pepper	1.2 mL
1 lb.	dried spaghetti	454 g

Heat the milk in a small pot until simmering. Add the bread, remove from the heat and stir until the bread becomes a paste. Cool. In a large bowl, combine the egg, beef, pork, Parmesan cheese, salt, pepper, parsley and the cooled bread paste. Mix well until it is thoroughly combined. Shape the mixture into 2-inch (5-cm) balls. You should have about 24 meatballs, give or take a few.

In a blender or food processor, purée the tomatoes, in batches if necessary. Press the tomato purée through a sieve to remove the seeds.

In a large heavy pot, heat the olive oil over medium. Add the prosciutto and cook until it darkens. Add the garlic and cook for a few moments, stirring. Add the onion and cook until it is translucent, 3-4 minutes. Add the tomato purée, paste, salt and pepper. Bring to a boil, then reduce to a simmer. Cook, stirring frequently, for 30 minutes.

While the sauce simmers, place the meatballs 1 inch (2.5 cm) apart on a baking sheet with a rim. Preheat the broiler and place the baking sheet 4-6 inches (10-15 cm) from the heat source. Broil until the meatballs are lightly browned on top. Turn the meatballs over and broil until lightly browned on the other side. Add the meatballs to the sauce and simmer for about 30 minutes longer, or until the sauce heavily coats the back of a spoon.

Bring a large pot of water to a boil. Salt liberally. Add the pasta and cook until it is tender but still firm to the bite. Drain. Divide the pasta among heated bowls and ladle the sauce and meatballs over each portion. Serve immediately.

Pork Tenderloin with Bourbon and Molasses

Serve with Lemon Roasted Sweet Potatoes, page 140.

Serves 6-8

1/4 cup	bourbon	60 mL
2 Tbsp.	molasses	30 mL
2 tsp.	whole grain mustard	10 mL
4	garlic cloves, minced	4
2 Tbsp.	shallots, finely chopped	30 mL
2 Tbsp.	vegetable oil	30 mL
1 tsp.	salt	5 mL
2 tsp.	coarsely crushed black pepper	10 mL
2-4	trimmed pork tenderloins, about 3 lbs. (1.4 kg)	2-4

Combine all ingredients except the meat in a dish big enough to hold the pork tenderloins. Roll the tenderloins in the marinade, making sure to coat them completely. Cover and refrigerate overnight.

Preheat the barbecue or broiler to high. Grill or broil the meat 4-5 minutes on each side for medium. Remove the tenderloins and let sit for a few minutes before slicing.

Grilled Pork Tenderloin with Hot and Sweet Spices

Serve the pork with rice and black beans. The tenderloins can be broiled or pan-roasted instead of grilled. This marinade can be used on chicken as well.

Serves 4

2-3	trimmed pork tenderloins, about 1 1/2 lbs. (680 g) in total	2-3
3/4 cup	red onion, chopped	180 mL
3/4 cup	green onion, thinly sliced	180 mL
2	jalapeño peppers, sliced	2
1/2 cup	vegetable oil	120 mL
1/2 cup	freshly squeezed orange juice	120 mL
2 Tbsp.	freshly squeezed lemon juice	30 mL
1/2 cup	soy sauce	120 mL
4 Tbsp.	fresh thyme leaves	60 mL
4	slices fresh ginger	4
1/2 tsp.	ground nutmeg	2.5 mL
1/2 tsp.	ground allspice	2.5 mL
1/2 tsp.	ground cinnamon	2.5 mL
1/2 tsp.	black pepper	2.5 mL
1 tsp.	salt	5 mL
1 Tbsp.	brown sugar	15 mL

Place the pork tenderloins between sheets of waxed pepper and pound lightly until the meat is slightly flattened. Place in a glass baking dish.

Combine the remaining ingredients in a blender or food processor and purée to a fine paste. Pour over the tenderloins and roll them around to coat them completely with the marinade. Cover and refrigerate overnight.

Preheat the barbecue over high heat. Grill the pork, 6-8 minutes per side for medium. Let sit for a few minutes before slicing.

Sausages with Polenta and Porcini Mushrooms

A few simple ingredients can make a great dish. If you don't have the time or patience for polenta, the sauce can be served over pasta. Porcini mushrooms, also known as cèpes, can be found in Italian delis and well-stocked supermarkets.

Serves 4

1 1/2 lbs.	sweet Italian sausage	680 g
1 oz.	dried porcini mushrooms	28 g
1 cup	boiling water	240 mL
1 Tbsp.	olive oil	15 mL
1/2 cup	onion, finely diced	120 mL
1/2 cup	red wine	120 mL
1	28-oz. (796-mL) can plum tomatoes, drained and finely chopped	1
	salt and pepper to taste	
10 cups	water	2.5 L
2 tsp.	salt	10 mL
2 cups	cornmeal	475 mL
6 Tbsp.	unsalted butter	90 mL
1 cup	freshly grated Parmesan cheese	240 mL

Soak the porcini mushrooms in the boiling water until soft. Examine the stem ends for sandy deposits and trim. Remove the mushrooms from the water and strain the soaking liquid through a coffee filter to remove the sand. Reserve the liquid.

Cut the sausage into 1-inch (2.5-cm) pieces. Heat the olive oil in a frying pan over medium heat. Add the sausages and sauté until brown. Remove the sausages and add the onion. Sauté until the onion is translucent. Return the sausage to the pan and add the red wine. Simmer until the wine is reduced by half. Add the porcini liquid and reduce by half. Add the tomatoes and porcini. Simmer until thickened, about 20 minutes. Season with salt and pepper and remove from the heat.

In a large, heavy-bottomed pot, bring the water to a boil. Add the salt, then stir in the cornmeal in a slow steady stream. Turn the heat to medium-low and cook at a lively simmer for 1 hour, stirring frequently. Stir in the butter and Parmesan cheese. Spread the polenta on a platter or into individual bowls. Reheat the sauce and spoon over the polenta.

Tourtière (for Norah)

I would love to say that this tourtière has been passed down to me from my great-great-grandmother, and eaten by my family on countless Christmas Eves, but I can't. Instead, it is the culmination of years of my own tourtière making. I like it best as a leftover, right out of the fridge. It's the kind of food that Steven declares is good to have while you are looking in the fridge, deciding what to eat.

Serves 6

2 1/2 lbs.	ground pork	1.1 kg
1 1/2 cups	onion, finely diced	360 mL
3 cups	water	720 mL
1 tsp.	salt	5 mL
1/4 tsp.	black pepper	1.2 mL
1 tsp.	ground dried ginger	5 mL
	large pinch of cinnamon	
1/2 tsp.	ground nutmeg	2.5 mL
1/4 tsp.	ground allspice	1.2 mL
1/8 tsp.	ground cloves	.5 mL
1/2 tsp.	dried thyme	2.5 mL
1/2-1 cup	fine dry breadcrumbs	120-240 mL
3 cups	all-purpose flour	720 mL
1/2 tsp.	salt	2.5 mL
9 oz.	lard	255 g
7 Tbsp.	cold water	105 mL
1	egg yolk	1
2 tsp.	water	10 mL

In a large nonstick or heavy pot, cook the pork and onion over medium heat, crumbling the pork with the back of a spoon, until it is cooked through. Transfer to a sieve to drain off the fat and return to the pot. Add the water, salt, pepper, ginger, cinnamon, nutmeg, allspice, cloves and thyme. Simmer over low heat, stirring occasionally, until the pork is tender, about 1 hour. The mixture should not be dry. Add a bit more water if you think it necessary while the pork is simmering.

Remove from the heat and stir in 1/2 cup (120 mL) of the breadcrumbs. Check the consistency. The pork mixture should be soft and flowing, with all of the liquid absorbed by the breadcrumbs. Use up to 1 cup (240 mL) of breadcrumbs if you think it necessary. Check the seasoning and adjust it, as the breadcrumbs will make the filling less zesty.

While the filling is cooking, make the crust. Combine the flour and salt in a large bowl. Cut the lard into 1/2-inch (1.2-cm) cubes and toss with the flour. Gently work the lard into the flour with your fingertips or a pastry blender until it forms pea-sized pieces. Pour in the chilled water and mix with your fingertips until it forms a loosely structured ball. There may be a few bits and pieces left in the bottom of the bowl—don't try to incorporate them. Wrap the dough in plastic wrap and keep in a cool place until you are ready to roll it out. The tourtière filling and the pastry may be made 2 days in advance. Wrap well and refrigerate.

Preheat the oven to 425°F (220°C). Remove the pastry and tourtière filling from the refrigerator and let them sit at room temperature for 1/2 hour to take the chill off if you have made them in advance. Divide the dough into two balls, one slightly larger than the other, and flatten out on a well-floured surface. Roll out the larger piece with a floured rolling pin to 1/4-inch (.6-cm) thickness. Roll the pastry around the pin as if you are rolling up a jelly roll and unroll over a 9-inch (23-cm) deep pie pan. Without stretching it, gently smooth and pat the dough into the pan.

Place the filling in the pan and smooth the top. Brush the rim lightly with water. Roll out the smaller piece of dough in the same manner as you rolled out the bottom and place over the top. Trim the edge to 1/2 inch (1.2 cm) and crimp in any way that pleases you. You can cut leaves out of the remaining dough and use them to decorate the top of the tourtière, gluing them on by lightly brushing the underside with water. Cut a V or a decorative pattern in the top to let the steam escape. Beat the egg yolk with the water and brush the top of the pie. Place on a tray (to catch any drips) and bake for 15 minutes. Reduce the heat to 375°F (190°C) and bake for 45-60 minutes, until the tourtière is a deep golden brown. Remove from the oven and let stand for 15 minutes before cutting.

Tomato, Fennel and Orzo Soup with Spicy Sausage

*A meal in a bowl—
the flavors develop if
it is allowed to sit
overnight.*

Serves 4-6

1 lb.	spicy Italian sausage, in natural casings cut into 1/2-inch (1.2-cm) slices	454 g
2 Tbsp.	olive oil	30 mL
1 cup	onion, finely diced	240 mL
2	cloves garlic, minced	2
1/2 cup	carrots, finely diced	120 mL
1/2 cup	celery, finely diced	120 mL
4 cups	chicken stock	1 L
1	28-oz. (796-mL) can Italian plum tomatoes with juice, puréed	1
1 Tbsp.	tomato paste	15 mL
1	fennel bulb, trimmed of stalks and blemishes, finely diced	1
	salt and pepper to taste	
3/4 cup	orzo, or other small pasta shapes	180 mL
2 cups	fresh spinach leaves, finely chopped	475 mL

In a large heavy pot, cook the sliced sausage over medium-low heat without oil until lightly browned on both sides. Remove the sausage from the pot and discard the fat. Add the olive oil to the pot and turn the heat to medium. Add the onion, garlic, carrots and celery. Cook, stirring frequently, until the onion is lightly browned. Add the chicken stock, puréed tomatoes, tomato paste and fennel.

Bring to a boil, turn down to a simmer, and cook for 1/2 hour, stirring occasionally. Taste and season with salt and pepper. Return the soup to a boil and add the sausage and orzo. Cook for 10-12 minutes, until the orzo is tender. Stir in the spinach and cook for 1 minute longer. Add a bit more water or stock if you find it too thick and adjust the seasoning. Serve in heated bowls.

Warm Lentil and Chicory Salad with Bacon Dressing

I like to add a drizzle of truffle oil to this salad for a true taste experience. It is very good, truffled or not, with roasted lamb rack or leg.

Serves 6

1/2 lb.	small brown lentils	227 g
1	large shallot, finely diced	1
2 Tbsp.	red wine vinegar	30 mL
1 tsp.	Dijon mustard	5 mL
3/4 tsp.	salt	4 mL
1/2 cup	olive oil	120 mL
1/4 lb.	sliced bacon, cut into 1-inch (2.5-cm) pieces	113 g
2 Tbsp.	fresh parsley, chopped	30 mL
1	large head chicory, washed, dried and torn into 1-inch (2.5-cm) pieces	1

Pick over the lentils and remove any stones or chaff. Rinse well. Place in a large pot and cover generously with water. Bring to a boil and skim off any foam that rises to the top. Turn down to a simmer and cook until the lentils are tender but not mushy.

While the lentils are cooking, make the vinaigrette. Combine the shallot, vinegar, Dijon mustard and salt in a bowl. Mix well. Slowly beat in the olive oil. Fry the bacon over medium heat until crisp and brown. Discard the fat. Keep the bacon in the frying pan.

Drain the lentils and combine with 2/3 of the vinaigrette and the parsley. Set aside for an hour or so.

When you are ready to serve the salad, toss the chicory with the remaining dressing and divide among 6 plates. Add the lentils to the bacon in the pan and heat quickly over high heat. Spoon the lentils over the greens and serve immediately.

Potato and Goat Cheese Cake with Rosemary

This stands well on its own, with an interesting salad or as an accompaniment to grilled steaks, or cut in small pieces on a buffet. Serve warm or at room temperature.

Serves 6

1 1/2 lbs.	small red potatoes	680 g
4 Tbsp.	unsalted butter, at room temperature	60 mL
1/4 lb.	soft, full-flavored goat cheese, crumbled	113 g
1/2 cup	sour cream	120 mL
2	large eggs	2
1/2 tsp.	salt	2.5 mL
1/2 tsp.	black pepper	2.5 mL
2 tsp.	fresh parsley, finely chopped	10 mL
1 tsp.	fresh rosemary, finely chopped	5 mL

Put the potatoes in a large pot, cover with cold water by 2 inches (5 cm), bring to a boil and cook until the potatoes are barely tender. They should be very firm and barely cooked in the center. Drain and cool.

Oil a 9-inch (23-cm) square baking dish and line with parchment paper or well-buttered, heavy-duty aluminum foil, allowing the ends to hang over the side for easy removal later. Preheat the oven to 375°F (190°C).

In a large bowl, cream the butter and goat cheese together. Beat in the sour cream, eggs, salt, pepper, parsley and rosemary. Slice the cooled potatoes into 1/4-inch (.6-cm) slices. Gently stir the potatoes into the goat cheese mixture. Transfer to the baking pan and gently smooth the top. Bake for 35-45 minutes, until the potatoes are tender when pierced with a knife. Place on a rack to cool. Lift the potato cake out of the pan and cut into pieces, discarding the foil or parchment paper.

Mashed Potatoes and Leeks
with Parmesan and Romano Cheese

*Fabulous with My
Meatloaf, page 35.*

A Bit About Leeks

*Growing leeks is a tedious
operation. They are grown in
trenches and soil is packed over
them as they grow to keep
them light in color. (This is why
leeks have to be washed well.
All that soil gets into the
crevices.) Depending upon the
skill and patience of the grower,
you can get a leek that has a
nice, long, edible white and
light green part or a short,
mean-spirited stub. I try to avoid
the stubs, but sometimes this is
all that is available. Anyway, use
the white and light green parts
of the leek and you will be just
fine. (I once worked with
someone who actually made a
soup out of the green leaves. It
was dreadful.)*

*To clean leeks, cut off the green
tops and remove the outer
covering. Thinly slice the leeks
and place them in a large bowl
of cold water. Swish the leeks
around with your hand to
dislodge any grit. Let stand for a
few minutes and remove the
leeks with a slotted spoon to a
sieve to drain. If you need
bigger pieces of leek, split them
in half lengthwise instead of
slicing them. Riffle the leaves
under cold running water until
they are free of grit, then drain.*

Serves 4-6

2 cups	leeks, white and light green part only, cut into 1-inch (2.5-cm) pieces	475 mL
1 1/2 lbs.	russet potatoes, peeled and cut into 1-inch (2.5-cm) pieces	680 g
3 Tbsp.	unsalted butter	45 mL
1/4 cup	warm milk	60 mL
1/2 cup	freshly grated Parmesan cheese	120 mL
1/4 cup	freshly grated Romano cheese	60 mL
	salt and pepper to taste	

Combine the leeks and potatoes in a large pot. Bring to a
boil and salt liberally. Cook until the potatoes are fork-
tender, 10-15 minutes.

Drain the vegetables and return to the pot. Mash until the
potatoes are completely smooth. Don't worry about the
pieces of leek—they add texture to the finished dish.
Mash in the butter and then beat in the warm milk with a
spoon. Stir in the cheeses and correct the seasoning.

Sweet Potato and Apple Purée with Bourbon

The bourbon gives a great "edge" to the potatoes. This goes especially well with pork.

Serves 8

5 lbs.	sweet potatoes or yams	2.3 kg
4	Granny Smith apples, cored	4
2 Tbsp.	unsalted butter	30 mL
1/4 cup	sour cream	60 mL
1/4 cup	brown sugar	60 mL
1/4 cup	bourbon	60 mL
	salt and pepper to taste	

Preheat the oven to 400°F (200°C). Prick the sweet potatoes with a fork and place them on a baking sheet. Place the apples in the middle of the potatoes. Roast for about an hour, until the potatoes and apples are completely tender. Check the apples after 1/2 hour and remove them if they are tender. Remove from the oven and cool for 15 minutes.

Cut the potatoes and apples in half and scoop out all the flesh. Either purée the potatoes and apples in a food processor or with a hand mixer, or mash them by hand, depending upon the texture you like. Place in a heavy pot. Stir in the butter until melted, then add the sour cream, brown sugar and bourbon. Season with salt and pepper. The dish can be made a day in advance. Cover and refrigerate. Warm over low heat until heated through.

Red Cabbage Braised with Maple Syrup

Very good with Hubert's Whole Roasted Veal Shanks, page 181.

Serves 4-6

2 Tbsp.	vegetable oil	30 mL
2 cups	onion, finely diced	475 mL
2	apples, peeled, cored and thinly sliced	2
2 lbs.	red cabbage, quartered, cored and thinly sliced crosswise	900 g
1/2 tsp.	salt	2.5 mL
1 cup	red wine	240 mL
1/2 cup	maple syrup	120 mL
1 Tbsp.	apple cider vinegar	15 mL
6	whole allspice berries	6
6	whole cloves	6
1	2-inch (5-cm) stick cinnamon, broken into small pieces	1
1 tsp.	apple cider vinegar	5 mL
	salt and pepper to taste	

Heat the vegetable oil in a large pot over medium heat. Add the onion and sauté until it is lightly browned. Add the apples and cabbage and cook, stirring frequently, until the cabbage is reduced in volume by half. Add the salt, wine, maple syrup and 1 Tbsp. (15 mL) vinegar. Tie the whole spices in a small piece of cheesecloth and add to the pot.

Cover and cook over the lowest heat, stirring occasionally, until all the liquid has evaporated and the cabbage is extremely tender, 1 1/2 -2 hours. Add the 1 tsp. (5 mL) vinegar and season with salt and pepper.

Lemon Risotto

Serves 4 as a side dish

An elegant risotto that will go nicely with fish, chicken and pork dishes.

3 cups	chicken stock	720 mL
1 Tbsp.	olive oil	15 mL
1/2 cup	onion, finely chopped	120 mL
1 cup	arborio rice	240 mL
	salt to taste	
3 Tbsp.	freshly squeezed lemon juice	45 mL
2 tsp.	lemon zest	10 mL
1 Tbsp.	unsalted butter	15 mL
1/4 cup	freshly grated Parmesan cheese	60 mL

Place chicken stock in a pot and bring to a simmer.

In a large heavy pot, heat the oil over medium heat. Add the onion and sauté until translucent but not browned. Add the rice and stir to coat it with the oil. Add 1/2 cup (120 mL) of the hot stock and stir until the liquid is absorbed and the rice is creamy. Continue stirring, adding the stock by half-cups until the rice is very firm. Season with salt. Continue adding stock until the rice is tender, creamy and slightly firm to the bite. Add the lemon juice, zest and butter. Adjust the seasoning and stir in the Parmesan cheese.

Baked Apples with Mascarpone and Amaretti

Mascarpone is the creamy mild cheese that became popular through the well-known dessert, tiramisu. Mascarpone and amaretti cookies are available in Italian delis and well-stocked supermarkets.

Serves 6

6	apples	6
2 Tbsp.	brown sugar	30 mL
1/4 tsp.	cinnamon	1.2 mL
1/2 cup	water	120 mL
1 cup	mascarpone	240 mL
6	amaretti cookies, crushed coarsely	6

Preheat the oven to 350°F (175°C). Core the apples and cut a strip from around the middle of each with a vegetable peeler. Place the apples in a baking pan that fits the apples snugly. Mix the brown sugar and cinnamon together and sprinkle into the apples. Pour the water around the apples and cover tightly. Bake for 1 hour, basting every 20 minutes, until the apples are tender.

While the apples are baking, mix the mascarpone and amaretti together.

Remove the apples from the oven and let rest for 10 minutes. Transfer to plates and fill the centers with the mascarpone mixture. Pour the syrup from the pan over the apples and serve warm.

Coconut and Dried Mango Bread Pudding

Winter is a good time to indulge in bread puddings and a taste of the tropics. Dried mangoes are available in natural food stores.

Makes 6 servings

1/2 lb.	good white bread, crusts removed, cut into 1-inch (2.5-cm) cubes	227 g
1/2 cup	sweetened, long-shred coconut	120 mL
1/2 cup	dried mango, finely diced	120 mL
1 cup	canned, sweetened coconut cream (such as Coco Lopez)	240 mL
1 1/4 cups	milk	300 mL
1/4 cup	sugar	60 mL
1/4 tsp.	salt	1.2 mL
3	large eggs	3
2 tsp.	pure vanilla extract	10 mL

Butter a 9- by 9-inch (23- by 23-cm) baking dish. Arrange half the bread cubes in the dish. Sprinkle with half the coconut and all the diced mango. Cover with the remaining bread cubes and sprinkle with the other half of the coconut.

Heat the coconut cream, milk, sugar and salt together over low heat until the sugar dissolves. Whisk the eggs together with the vanilla. Whisk the warm milk mixture into the eggs. Pour over the bread and let sit for 1/2 hour.

Preheat the oven to 350°F (175°C). Bake until the pudding is set and golden brown on the top, 40-50 minutes. Transfer to a rack and cool slightly. Serve with whipped cream if desired.

Chocolate, Croissant and Almond Bread Pudding with Bourbon Whipped Cream

This is what happens when croissants go to heaven.

Serves 6

4	large croissants	4
8 oz.	bittersweet chocolate, chopped into 1/2-inch (1.2-cm) chunks	227 g
4 oz.	almond paste, chopped into 1/4-inch (.6-cm) chunks	113 g
5	large egg yolks	5
1/4 cup	sugar	60 mL
1 tsp.	pure vanilla extract	5 mL
2 cups	half-and-half cream	475 mL
1 1/2 cups	whipping cream	360 mL
1 Tbsp.	icing sugar	15 mL
2 Tbsp.	bourbon	30 mL

Preheat the oven to 350°F (175°C).

Cut the croissants in half and toast them until golden brown. Tear into 1/2-inch (1.2-cm) pieces and place in a 9-inch-square (23-cm) deep baking dish.

Evenly distribute the chocolate and almond paste over the croissants. Beat the egg yolks, sugar and vanilla together. Heat the light cream to just below boiling and whisk it into the egg yolks. Pour the mixture over the croissants. Cover tightly with aluminum foil and place in a larger pan. Pour enough boiling water into the outer pan so that it comes halfway up the side of the baking dish. Bake for 30-35 minutes or until just set. Remove from the water bath, remove the foil and cool.

Whip the cream and icing sugar until soft peaks form. Stir in the bourbon and serve the whipped cream with the pudding.

Banana Chocolate Espresso Brazil Nut Cake

For the best flavor, this cake is aged overnight before serving.

Makes 1 10-inch (25-cm) cake

1 1/4 cups	flour	300 mL
1 cup	cocoa (not Dutch-process)	240 mL
1 tsp.	baking soda	5 mL
1/2 tsp.	salt	2.5 mL
1 Tbsp.	instant coffee	15 mL
1 Tbsp.	hot water	15 mL
2	extremely ripe bananas, mashed	2
1/2 cup	sour cream	120 mL
1 tsp.	pure vanilla extract	5 mL
1/2 cup	unsalted butter at room temperature	120 mL
1 cup	granulated sugar	240 mL
1/2 cup	light brown sugar, packed	120 mL
2	large eggs	2
1 1/2 cups	Brazil nuts, coarsely chopped	360 mL

Preheat the oven to 350°F (175°C). Butter and flour a 10-inch (25-cm) bundt pan.

Sift the flour, cocoa, baking soda and salt together. Set aside. Dissolve the instant coffee in the hot water. Combine with the bananas, sour cream and vanilla. Set aside.

In a large bowl, cream the butter by hand or with an electric mixer. Add both sugars and beat until fluffy. Beat in the eggs one at a time. Add the flour mixture and banana mixture alternately in three additions, beating only until combined. Stir in the Brazil nuts.

Scrape the batter into the prepared pan and smooth the top. Bake for 50 minutes, until a cake tester inserted into the middle comes out clean. Cool for 10 minutes in the pan, then turn out onto a rack to cool completely. Wrap tightly in plastic wrap and let sit overnight before serving.

Banana, Honey and Walnut Upside-Down Cake

Serve slightly warm with Lemon Curd, page 54, or sour cream.

Makes 1 9-inch (23-cm) cake

1/4 cup	unsalted butter	60 mL
1/4 cup	liquid honey	60 mL
1 cup	golden brown sugar, packed	240 mL
1/2 cup	walnut halves	120 mL
4	large bananas, cut diagonally into 1/4-inch (.6-cm) slices	4
1 cup	all-purpose flour	240 mL
2 tsp.	baking powder	10 mL
1/2 tsp.	cinnamon	2.5 mL
1/4 tsp.	nutmeg	1.2 mL
1/4 tsp.	salt	1.2 mL
6 Tbsp.	unsalted butter, at room temperature	90 mL
3/4 cup	sugar	180 mL
1	large egg	1
1/2 tsp.	pure vanilla extract	2.5 mL
6 Tbsp.	milk	90 mL

Preheat the oven to 325°F (165°C).

Put the unsalted butter in a 9-inch (23-cm) round baking pan and place in the oven until the butter melts. Remove from the oven, and drizzle the honey and sprinkle the brown sugar over the butter. Arrange the walnuts and then the bananas over the brown sugar.

Whisk the flour, baking powder, cinnamon, nutmeg and salt together. Cream the butter and sugar together by hand or with an electric mixer until light and fluffy. Beat in the egg and vanilla. Add the flour mixture and milk alternately in three additions, beating only until combined. Scrape the batter over the bananas and gently smooth the top. Bake until a tester comes out clean, 45-55 minutes. Cool on a rack for 1/2 hour, then invert onto a plate.

Chocolate Lava Cake

This is called lava cake because the delicious, oozy chocolate center runs out onto the plate when you cut into the cake. People go wild over this dessert. One of the most popular desserts at the Fish House in Stanley Park, where it was born.

Makes 6 Servings

6 1/2 oz.	good-quality bittersweet chocolate, chopped into 1/2-inch (1.2-cm) pieces	185 g
3 Tbsp.	unsalted butter	45 mL
	pinch of salt	
4	large egg yolks	4
1/4 cup	granulated sugar	60 mL
2	large egg whites	2
	butter at room temperature for buttering the pans	
	cocoa powder for dusting the pans	
1 recipe	Coffee Crème Anglaise	1 recipe

Assemble six 4- by 2-inch (10- by 5-cm) nonstick tart pans, preferably smooth-sided with removable bottoms, or six 4-inch (10-cm) disposable aluminum pie pans. Thoroughly butter the insides of the pans and dust with cocoa. Tap out the excess.

Combine the chocolate, unsalted butter and pinch of salt in a large, heatproof bowl. Place over a pot of simmering water and stir occasionally until the chocolate is almost completely melted. Remove from the heat and stir until the chocolate is smooth. Cool to room temperature.

Combine the egg yolks with all but 1 Tbsp. (15 mL) of the sugar and beat with an electric mixer or by hand at high speed for about 2 minutes, until the mixture thickens and becomes lighter in color. Fold the cooled chocolate mixture into the egg yolks until smoothly combined.

With clean beaters, whip the egg whites with the remaining 1 Tbsp. (15 mL) of sugar until soft peaks form. Stir 1/3 of the egg whites into the chocolate mixture. Fold the remaining egg whites into the chocolate mixture.

Spoon the batter into the prepared tart tins. If you are not baking the Lava Cakes immediately, cover with plastic wrap and refrigerate for up to 8 hours.

Preheat the oven to 425°F (220°C). Place the cakes well apart on a baking sheet and bake for 8 minutes, or 9 minutes if the cakes have been refrigerated. The centers will be jiggly. Remove from the oven and carefully loosen the tarts with a small knife. Flip the cakes over onto individual plates and remove the pans.

Serve with Coffee Crème Anglaise, below, poured around the Lava Cakes, and unsweetened whipped cream if you wish.

Coffee Crème Anglaise

This is good with any kind of chocolate dessert.

Makes 2 1/2 cups (600 mL)

5	large egg yolks	5
1/2 cup	granulated sugar	120 mL
2 cups	half-and-half cream	480 mL
1 tsp.	instant coffee	5 mL
1 Tbsp.	espresso coffee beans, coarsely ground	15 mL

In a large bowl, beat the egg yolks and sugar together with an electric mixer until thick and light in color, about 2 minutes.

Place the cream in a heavy saucepan and bring just to a boil. Remove from the heat and slowly pour 1/4 of the cream into the yolk mixture, stirring constantly, then stir the yolk mixture into the remaining cream in the pot. Set the pot over medium-low heat and stir constantly with a rubber spatula until the mixture thickens. To test, remove the pot from the heat and dip a metal spoon into the cream. Draw your finger across the back of the spoon through the cream. If the track of your finger remains, it is ready. Remove from the heat immediately and pour through a sieve into a clean bowl. Stir in the instant coffee until dissolved, then the coarsely ground espresso beans. Place in the fridge and stir every 10 minutes until the mixture is cold. Cover with plastic wrap. Keeps for 4 days, refrigerated.

Buttered Rum and Raisin Cake

Broil day-old slices of this cake and serve warm with coffee ice cream.

Makes 1 8-inch (20-cm) cake

1/4 cup	dark rum	60 mL
1/2 cup	golden raisins	120 mL
1/2 cup	granulated sugar	120 mL
1 Tbsp.	water	15 mL
1/4 cup	water	60 mL
3 Tbsp.	unsalted butter, softened	45 mL
2 Tbsp.	dark rum	30 mL
1 cup	all-purpose flour	240 mL
1 1/4 tsp.	baking powder	6.2 mL
1/4 tsp.	nutmeg	1.2 mL
1/4 tsp.	salt	1.2 mL
1/2 cup plus 2 Tbsp.	unsalted butter	150 mL
3/4 cup	light brown sugar, firmly packed	180 mL
3	large eggs	3
1 tsp.	pure vanilla extract	5 mL
1/2 cup	walnuts, coarsely chopped	120 mL

In a small pot, bring the rum to a boil. Add the raisins, remove from the heat and cover. Let stand for 1 hour.

In a small pot combine the granulated sugar and the 1 Tbsp. (15 mL) water. Bring to a boil and cook over high heat until the sugar caramelizes and is almost smoking. Remove from the heat and place a sieve over the top of the pot. Stand back from the pot and add the 1/4 cup (60 mL) water. The caramel will splutter. When it stops spluttering, remove the sieve and stir in the 3 Tbsp. (45 mL) unsalted butter until melted. Stir in the 2 Tbsp. (30 mL) rum. Set aside.

Preheat the oven to 350°F (175°C). Butter and flour an 8-inch (20-cm) deep round cake pan. Whisk the flour, baking powder, nutmeg and salt together in a bowl. With an electric mixer, beat the butter until light and fluffy. Gradually add the brown sugar and beat for 1 minute. Beat in the eggs one at a time, then the vanilla. On low speed, blend in the flour mixture, then the rum-soaked raisins and the walnuts. Scrape the batter into the cake

pan and smooth the top. Bake for 35-45 minutes, or until a tester comes out clean. Remove from the oven and cool on a rack for 5 minutes. Run a knife around the edge of the pan and lift the cake. Place back in the pan. With a skewer, poke about 15 holes through the cake. Slowly spoon the caramel sauce over the top. Let stand until cool before removing from the pan.

Pineapple Custard Flan

I love creamy desserts like this one. It can be served warm or at room temperature. The pineapple adds a nice contrast to the smoothness of the custard. If I was a child, I would probably eat it with Nice cookies (hint, hint)!

Serves 6

2 cups	fresh pineapple, cut into 1-inch (1.2-cm) cubes	475 mL
3	large eggs	3
3	large egg yolks	3
2 Tbsp.	all-purpose flour	30 mL
2/3 cup	sugar	160 mL
1 cup	milk	240 mL
1 cup	half-and-half cream	240 mL
1 tsp.	pure vanilla extract	5 mL
2 Tbsp.	brown sugar	30 mL

Preheat the oven to 400°F (200°C). Butter a 10-inch (25-cm) round glass or ceramic baking dish. Spread the pineapple chunks in an even layer in the baking dish. Bake for 35 minutes, stirring halfway through, and remove from the oven.

Beat the eggs, egg yolks, flour and sugar together. Beat in the milk, cream and vanilla. Pour over the pineapple. Reduce the oven temperature to 350°F (175°C) and place the baking dish in a larger pan. Pour hot water in the outer pan to come halfway up the side of the baking dish. Bake in the middle of the oven for 30-40 minutes until the custard is just set. It should barely jiggle in the middle. Cool in the water bath to room temperature. Before serving, sprinkle the top of the custard with the brown sugar. Broil until the sugar is bubbly.

Basics and Biscuits

Chicken Stock

I like to make a plain chicken stock with very little seasoning in it, so it can be used in many different dishes. It is worth your while to make a lot and freeze it in convenient portions in Zip-loc bags.

Makes 8-10 cups (2-2.4 L)

5 lbs.	chicken bones	2.3 kg
2	small onions, peeled and cut in half	2
2	small carrots, peeled and cut in half	2
2	celery stalks, cut in half	2
1	head garlic, cut in half crosswise	1
	water	

Put the chicken bones in a large stock pot. Cover with water and bring to a boil. Drain the bones in a colander and rinse with cold water. Return to the pot and add the remaining ingredients. Add water to cover by 4 inches (10 cm). Bring to a boil, turn down to a simmer and cook for 6 hours, skimming the top of fat. Add water periodically to return it to its original level. Strain through a cheesecloth-lined colander and cool. It will keep for 2-3 days refrigerated. Freeze for longer storage.

Stove-Top Roasted Garlic

This is easier than oven roasting whole bulbs but you won't have the pleasure of squeezing them from their skins. Use these in mashed potatoes, sauces, vinaigrettes or as a garnish for meat, fish or fowl. Use the oil for cooking or vinaigrettes.

Makes 2-3 cups (500-720 mL)

| 4 | large heads garlic | 4 |
| | olive or vegetable oil | |

Choose impeccably fresh, firm heads of garlic with no green sprouts. Separate the heads into cloves and peel them. Place the peeled cloves in a small heavy pot or frying pan and cover generously with the oil. Place on the stove over medium-low heat. As soon as bubbles form around the cloves, turn the heat to low and cook until they are golden brown and completely soft. This will take anywhere from 20-40 minutes.

Remove from the heat and cool completely. Transfer the garlic and oil to a clean container and store covered in the refrigerator. It will keep for 1 month.

Crème Fraîche

Crème fraîche is cultured cream, similar to sour cream, with all the properties of whipping cream.

Makes 2 cups (475 mL)

| 1/2 cup | sour cream | 120 mL |
| 1 1/2 cups | whipping cream | 360 mL |

In a large bowl whisk the sour cream briefly to loosen it up. Slowly whisk in the whipping cream to blend thoroughly without whipping. Cover and keep in a warm place overnight. Transfer to a storage container and refrigerate overnight before using. Crème fraîche will keep for 3-4 weeks refrigerated and gets better with age.

Crème fraîche can be heated or reduced without breaking up (as sour cream does), or whipped like whipping cream. It seems to thicken up more quickly than whipping cream, so I prefer to use a whisk rather than an electric mixer. It gives me more control over the results.

Flaky Pastry

Prebaking a Pie Shell

Preheat the oven to 400°F (200°C). Roll the pastry out to 1/4 inch (.5 cm) thickness, 3 inches (7.5 cm) larger than your pan. Roll the pastry around the rolling pin and unroll over the pan. Fit it gently into the corners and trim flush with the edge of the pan if you are using a tart pan. If you are using a pie pan, trim the overlap to 1 inch (2.5 cm), turn it under and crimp. Prick the bottom and sides lightly with a fork. Line the pan with a piece of aluminum foil large enough to protrude well over the edge. Fill it half-full with dried rice, beans or pie weights. Bake on the middle shelf of the oven for 15 minutes. Remove the foil and weights and bake another 5-10 minutes until the shell is pale gold.

Makes a 9- or 10-inch (23- or 25-cm) pie or tart

2 cups	all-purpose flour	475 mL
1/2 tsp.	salt	2.5 mL
3/4 cup	unsalted butter, well chilled	180 mL
1/3 cup	ice-cold water	80 mL

Combine the flour and salt in a large bowl. Cut the butter into 1/2-inch (1.2-cm) cubes and place on a plate in the freezer for 5 minutes.

Toss the chilled butter with the flour. Add the water and knead gently with your fingertips until the mixture forms a shaggy ball. Do not try to incorporate the flour that remains in the bottom of the bowl. Use immediately, or wrap and refrigerate for up to 3 days.

Buttermilk Biscuits

My father worked in what was then the "Italian district" of Ottawa when I was growing up. He discovered that a store in the area sold ricotta cheese that arrived fresh every Wednesday and brought some home. I was instantly smitten by its ultra-milky flavor and soft grainy texture. I would eat it spread on nasty (in retrospect) tea biscuits that my mother brought home from the weekly shopping trip, with a layer of Lyle's Golden Syrup spread on top. These biscuits would better honor the tradition of ricotta with Lyle's Golden Syrup, but on second thought, they might not.

Makes 8 biscuits

2 cups	all-purpose flour	475 mL
2 tsp.	baking powder	10 mL
1/2 tsp.	baking soda	2.5 mL
1/2 tsp.	salt	2.5 mL
1/4 cup	chilled unsalted butter	60 mL
1/4 cup	chilled vegetable shortening	60 mL
3/4 cup	chilled buttermilk	180 mL

Preheat the oven to 425°F (220°C). Sift the flour, baking powder, baking soda and salt into a bowl. Cut in the butter and shortening until it is mealy. Add the buttermilk and stir quickly with a fork until the mixture forms a dough.

Dump the dough out onto a floured surface, knead gently 5-6 times, and pat it out to 1/2-inch (1.2-cm) thickness. Cut out as many rounds as you can with a 3-inch (7.5-cm) cutter and place them on an ungreased baking sheet, 2 inches (5 cm) apart. Gently press the edges of the remaining scraps together and cut out more rounds. If you want, just cut the dough into 3-inch (7.5-cm) squares or diamonds. Bake on the middle rack of the oven until they are a pale gold, 12-15 minutes.

Instant Ecstasy Chocolate Cookies

While I am not too fond of chocolate desserts, I do love chocolate bars, cookies, brownies and just plain chocolate. These cookies satisfy all of the above requirements.

Makes 22 very large cookies

4 oz.	unsweetened chocolate, coarsely chopped	113 g
8 oz.	semisweet chocolate, coarsely chopped	227 g
1/2 cup	unsalted butter, at room temperature	120 mL
6 Tbsp.	all-purpose flour	90 mL
1/2 tsp.	baking powder	1.2 mL
1/2 tsp.	salt	1.2 mL
3	large eggs	3
1 cup	sugar	240 mL
1 Tbsp.	instant coffee powder	15 mL
1 Tbsp.	pure vanilla extract	15 mL
2 cups	pecan halves	475 mL
1 cup	whole almonds, roasted	240 mL
8 oz.	large chocolate chips or chocolate chunks	227 g

Preheat the oven to 300°F (150°C).

In a heatproof bowl, combine the unsweetened chocolate, semisweet chocolate and unsalted butter. Place over a pot of simmering water, stirring occasionally until melted. Remove from the heat and cool.

Whisk the flour, baking powder and salt together. Set aside.

With an electric mixer or whisk, beat the eggs and sugar together until light and fluffy. Add the coffee powder, vanilla and cooled chocolate mixture. Add the flour mixture and mix until combined. Fold in the nuts and chocolate chips or chunks.

Scoop out the batter using a 1/4-cup (60-mL) measure. Place 3 inches (7.5 cm) apart on parchment-lined baking sheets. Depending on the size of your baking sheets, you should be able to get 4-6 cookies on each sheet. Bake for 20 minutes, turning the sheets around halfway through, until the tops begin to crack. Be careful not to overbake. Let the cookies remain on the baking sheet for a minute or so to firm up, then transfer to a cooling rack.

Peanut Butter Cookies

I wanted a peanut butter cookie that was rich, crumbly and smooth with an intense peanut butter taste. Through experimenting, I found that replacing some of the flour with cornstarch and using a homogenized peanut butter gave the best result. Great with a big glass of milk.

Makes about 35 cookies

1 cup	flour	240 mL
1/2 tsp.	baking powder	2.5 mL
1/2 tsp.	baking soda	2.5 mL
1/2 cup	cornstarch	120 mL
1/2 tsp.	salt	2.5 mL
3/4 cup	unsalted butter	180 mL
1 cup	light brown sugar, well-packed	240 mL
1/2 cup	granulated sugar	120 mL
1	large egg	1
1 1/2 cups	homogenized peanut butter	360 mL

Sift the flour, baking powder, baking soda, cornstarch and salt together. By hand or with an electric mixer, cream the butter. Add the sugars and beat until light and fluffy. Beat in the egg, then the peanut butter until well combined. Stir in the flour mixture by hand. Cover the dough with plastic wrap and refrigerate until firm, about half an hour or up to 2 days.

Preheat the oven to 350°F (175°C). Butter two cookie sheets or line them with parchment paper. Scoop up heaping tablespoons of the dough and roll into balls. Place about 2 inches (5 cm) apart on the cookie sheets and flatten with the back of a fork to about 1/4 inch (.6 cm). Bake for 12-14 minutes, turning the cookie sheets around halfway through to ensure even browning. Place on a cooling rack until the cookies are firm enough to remove from the pan.

Index

Index

Index

Index

Index

Index

About the Author

*W*hen I was around nine, my mother taught me how to make omelettes and bake bread. The "Galloping Gourmet" taught me how to chop when I was ten, via TV. I read my mother's cookbooks avidly and tried different things—I fondly remember a meatloaf roulade with a cheddar cheese filling. My sister Jennifer had brought a friend home for dinner who was totally intimidated by this meatloaf creation. She looked miserable when confronted with it on her plate, and I could tell that she thought we were pretty weird because of the strange food we were eating. I thought it was a triumph of high cuisine.

The first foray out of recipe land was a disaster. I somehow got it into my head that I wanted to make an oxtail soup. I imagined it as being rich, decadent and sumptuous. I actually bought the oxtails with my allowance and came home full of excitement and hope. Visions of a rich brown soup danced in my head. I brewed up the oxtails, added barley and vegetables and, for some reason that is lost to me now, a handful of pickling spices. Of course I didn't realize that the oxtails would take hours to cook, barley would expand about three times and that pickling spices were not a common soup seasoning. I ended up with a pale barley sludge with tough bits of meat and the overpowering flavor and crunch of pickling spice. Everybody had a small, small bowl, saying it was not that bad, but I knew it was real bad. I persevered and continued to follow recipes to which I made slight changes until I felt comfortable enough to go solo.

◆ ◆ ◆

Karen Barnaby has worked as a chef for the past 20 years. Her favorite recipes range from Oysters Baked in Garlic and Sherry to the chocolate cake on the back of the Christie Chocolate Wafers box. Karen is currently the executive chef at the Fish House in Stanley Park, Vancouver. She is the author of *Pacific Passions Cookbook,* and co-author of the *David Wood Food Book* and the *David Wood Dessert Book.* She lives in Vancouver with her husband Steven and their two Dobermann pinschers, Ginger and Io. Her birthday really is on April 1.